Empower Yourself!

Empower Yourself!

A Take-Charge Assistant Book

Dr. Marlene Caroselli

AMACOM
American Management Association

New York • Atlanta • Boston • Chicago • Kansas City • San Fancisco • Washington, D.C.
Brussels • Mexico City • Tokyo • Toronto

This publication is designed to provide accurate and authoritative information in regard to the subject matter covered. It is sold with the understanding
that the publisher is not engaged in rendering legal, accounting, or other
professional service. If legal advice or other expert assistance is required, the
services of a competent professional person should be sought.

Library of Congress Cataloging-in-Publication Data

Caroselli, Marlene.
    Empower yourself!: a take-charge assistant book/Marlene
  Caroselli.
        p. cm.
Includes bibliographical references and index.
ISBN 0-8144-7951-0
1. Secretaries. 2. Career development. 3. Success in business.
I. Title.
HF5547.5.C353 1998
650.1'088'651—dc21   97-18762
                                                                      CIP

Printing number

10 9 8 7 6 5 4 3 2 1

Contents

4 Maintaining Composure

5 Grounding Yourself Against Future Shock

Acknowledgments

To Trish Rintels, Linda Edison, and Germaine Froehlich, with gratitude for serving as a panel of experts in this and so many other endeavors.

Empower Yourself!

Introduction

This is a book for the secretary who wants to take charge, for the assistant who welcomes responsibility, the clerk who regards challenge as opportunity. This is *not* a book for the faint of heart, for someone content to keep her talents hidden beneath a bushel or who wants the "status" to remain "quo" forever.

The empowered assistant gets things done because she is in charge. To suggest otherwise is to imply helplessness, hopelessness, and no empowerment at all. Rather than accept a victim mentality, I want you to assume a can-do confidence, a power posture, and an achievement attitude. In truth, just as we are all managers—of our own jobs at least—we are also in charge—of our jobs, our goals, our accomplishments.

Power, they say, does not flow to invisible people. As an empowered assistant, you know this. You do not hesitate to take risks or responsibility in order to get results. You have been able to move beyond the negative associations of the word *power* and to view instead the positive associations implied in the shift of *power* as a noun to *empowered* as an adjective.

In Chapter 1, you will learn how to establish authority so that you can proceed to establish a presence in the minds of others. By following the suggestions, working on the exercises, and studying the behaviors of other outstanding secretaries, you will be able to position yourself to have more clout—not in the aggrandizing sense of the word but in the sense that is required to get things done.

Once you have the authority to do things, you can begin to structure your own assignments. Chapter 2 tells you how to analyze tasks, develop teamwork, establish partnerships, and hone your problem-solving and decision-making skills. It too offers advice from a professional like yourself, a woman whose accomplishments are due in large measure to her organizational skills.

Chapter 3 presents communicating techniques used by top-notch professionals in situations ranging from persuasive to urgent, from small group meetings to large group presentations. You will learn how to determine your communication style and how to adapt it to various situations. You will also benefit from the advice of another empowered assistant, willing to share the secrets of her success.

Is there any assistant, anywhere in America, who has not been asked to do more with less? Probably not. The "less" (less time, fewer people, fewer resources) often means more—more stress and more managers to work for. How to maintain composure (or at least convince others that you are maintaining it) is the focus of Chapter 4. Specific composure destroyers, such as information overload, stress, grapevines, and conflicts, are examined. At the end of this chapter, two executive assistants share their ideas for remaining poised when the earth is quaking beneath your feet.

What can you do today to prepare yourself for tomorrow? How can you become "grounded" so you will not be shocked by the future? Chapter 5 offers suggestions that will help you enjoy change and acknowledge that when you're through changing, you're through. At the end of the chapter, you will hear from a technocrat, who will open a window to the future for you.

When we pull courage into ourselves, we are "encouraged." And when we pull joy into ourselves, we learn to "enjoy." Pulling power into ourselves allows us, in much the same way, to become "empowered." Once you've experienced the thrill of empowered victory, you will never again wish upon yourself the agony of defeat.

1

Establishing Authority

Changing Times, Changing Styles

There was a time in America, not so long ago, when supervisors supervised according to the command-and-control style. And when they spoke, everybody listened. Today, when *employees* talk, *supervisors* listen—at least the smart ones do. Employees have become empowered, teams allowed to self-direct, and many decisions pushed down to the lowest possible level.

Amid the change in the nanosecond nineties, marvelous opportunities are springing up. Opportunities abound to see and be seen, to recognize and be recognized, to take risk and to risk taking steps out of the rut of rigidity. Propelling these exciting events are people like management guru Tom Peters, who asserts on a brochure advertising a seminar, "If you have gone a whole week without being disobedient, you are doing yourself and your organization a disservice!" Imagine that! The "disobedience," of course, is not a willful breaking of laws but rather a willingness to question the way things are done in order to bring about continuous improvement.

What is turning tradition into turbulence, solo efforts into synergy, organization charts into organized chaos? A number of forces are exerting pressure on the old structures, converting pyramids into clover-leaf decentralization or "pizza pie" shapes with multiple, localized sources of power.

The *quality movement* is one such force, with its recognition that those closest to the process usually know it best. Quality gurus stress that all work is process, and when the processes are combined, the job in its entirety is defined. The combined processes constitute the system, or the way the work is done. Because the people engaged in the process usually know the process best of all, the best ideas for improvement ordinarily come from them.

We have been taught that the person who receives the output of our work is our customer. That means the customer could be someone in our organization—a manager or someone in shipping or someone who reads the report we

3

prepare. Or the customer could be outside the company. Whoever our work is done for is the customer.

Another force is *technology*, which has democratized offices. No longer is information for the privileged few. Thanks to the Internet, we can all obtain knowledge easily and inexpensively, thus flattening the curve of learning as far as time is concerned.

Finally, internationally recognized *experts* are advocating a shift in terms of who holds power, and from whom we can expect valuable contributions. A recent article in the *Washington Post* described an "agile company" (also called an "intelligent enterprise"). In such "virtual" companies, a few executives work in concert with administrative assistants, regarded as critically important components in these newly structured organizations. In a virtual company, most of the work is outsourced, but not the work of the administrative assistants.

In *Managers as Mentors*, author Chip Bell discusses upward mobility, which, he asserts, requires teaching, guiding, and mentoring. (Are these tasks that an empowered assistant can do? Absolutely.) Peter Block, in his best-selling *Stewardship*, encourages managers to serve rather than to control. He says, "No one should be able to make a living simply planning, watching, controlling, or evaluating the actions of others." A similar message is found in the popular book, *The Real Heroes of Business and Not a CEO Among Them*.

As supervisors are liberated from the confines of obsolete managing styles, so are employees, who now can work alongside rather than as subordinates to their managers. Uncountable opportunities are cropping up for secretaries who are willing to reach out and grab them. Think about this: Not very long ago, managers wouldn't be caught dead with their fingers on a keyboard. Now we see it all the time. Most supervisors in the precomputer era would pass proofreading tasks to their secretaries. Not any longer. Gone are the days when secretaries were counted on to make coffee and take notes. Today they run team meetings, benchmark, make presentations to senior management, pass out their own business cards, subscribe to their own journals (at least eight of them exist), and earn degrees. The very fact that the American *Management* Association has a large business unit dealing with secretaries is telling us that the lines that once separated managerial work from secretarial work are becoming blurred. In fact, a recent survey in the *Wall Street Journal* found 71 percent of secretaries reporting that many of their tasks are managerial in nature. And time management experts tell us 90 percent of the phone calls coming in to an office can be handled by a competent secretary.

Think of all the work that has to be done (by you *and* by your boss) as a huge blend of tasks. Imagine it all thrown together in a giant milkshake of responsibility. Is your straw long enough to reach the bottom, where the richest ingredients usually settle?

The Milkshake of Job Responsibilities

→ fluff stuff

→ blended tasks

→ most weighty ingredients

The "fluff stuff" represents surface and perhaps even superficial duties. They are important, but do not require much thought: filing, filling out forms, and record keeping, for example. In the middle are equally exchangeable tasks—ones that both the supervisor and the assistant are capable of doing, particularly if each is equally proficient on the computer. At the bottom are the "solid" and "heavy" requirements that the boss alone typically knows how to do.

Assistants who plan to move ahead are developing longer and longer straws to ensure they get at the "good stuff on the bottom." Considering the fact that since 1987, more than a half-million secretarial positions have disappeared, it is time for secretaries to think about what the future holds. Futurists predict that the secretarial role is headed in two directions: up and down. Up means that secretaries will function as administrative assistants in virtual offices and earn more than they do now. Down means some secretaries will wind up in primarily clerical roles, doing work that does not require much thought and consequently work that does not offer much in the way of financial remuneration. As *The Wall Street Journal* proclaimed several years back (May 10, 1993), because middle managers are being turned out and voice mail turned on, "secretaries are shouldering more responsibility for running the show" (p. A1). The article also bemoans the fact that although responsibility has increased, salaries have not. Since the mid-eighties, salaries have risen a scant 5 percent. The average secretary is earning about $25,000 a year.

There are those who believe that if they bury their head in the metaphorical sand, they can protect themselves from the winds of change. But think of what is exposed, what is most vulnerable when you are in that position. To CYA (cover your anatomy), you absolutely must regard change as inevitable and as a force that will provide you opportunities to enrich your life.

Using the 5-*In* Model

The time is ripe for secretaries to step out of constraining roles and up to the line where responsibilities and rewards are being passed out. One technique that will enable you to take charge of a given project is the 5-*In* Model.

The first "In" is *inform*. This means you have done the research on a project or topic, and your responsibility ends when you inform your supervisor of the findings. He takes over at this point and sees the project through to completion. This is the lowest level of empowerment and, clearly, a good place to start if you are new to the game of assuming greater responsibility.

When you are operating at the second level of empowerment, you *investigate*, meaning you go beyond data acquisition. You are now moving up the ladder a notch. Here, you make a recommendation to your supervisor, based on what you have researched. Of course, he is free to reject your recommendation, but you have at least placed the mantle of responsibility on your shoulders.

At the third level, *intend*, you have put your arms through the mantle's sleeves, so to speak. You have taken on a task and researched it well. You now determine what you intend to do to solve the problem or move forward with the project. When you are empowered enough to operate at this level, you are demonstrating that much trust has been placed in you. You still need your boss's approval to bring the project to completion, but you are very much in charge. Your boss can still suggest or modify or even tell you not to proceed, but you are tipping the scales to the point of equilibrium.

The fourth level, *initiate*, finds you in nearly complete charge of a project. You can initiate projects without needing approval, although you will need to keep your boss informed through periodic progress reports. At this level, you and your boss are operating as partners.

When you reach the final level in the model, you are *independent*. Your boss has worked with you long enough to know the quality of your work. He trusts you enough to assign you a project to handle from inception to completion without having to check with him on all the minor details. When you complete the project, you share the results with your boss, but there is no need to provide regular reports.

Do not expect to begin at the independent level. The development of trust is a lengthy process. As your boss learns more and more about your capability, he will be willing to turn more and more authority over to you.

Here is a sample dialogue that may prove useful as you are preparing for your first empowerment meeting with your boss.

Inform—Level 1

In the following dialogue, it is obvious the boss has not yet developed faith in the employee's talents. It is indeed appropriate for the assistant to start at this level. Once she has gathered the information she needs, she will present it to her boss, who will make the decision of whether to proceed with the program. Because the boss will take charge at this point, it is altogether possible that any success the program has will ultimately be accorded to her. Expect this to happen at this level. It is part of paying one's dues.

> ASSISTANT. Thank you, Jeannette, for taking the time to meet with me today. I won't need more than a few minutes to outline a proposal to you—one for a series of lunchtime lectures.

> BOSS. What in the world are lunchtime lectures?

> ASSISTANT. They are lectures on work-related topics held during the lunch hour so that there is no loss of company time. I heard they are holding them at R. Competitor's, and it seemed like a good idea to try here.

Boss. What's it going to cost?

Assistant. That's what I need to find out. But if you have no objections, I'd like to make a few calls, gather some data, and then report back to you on my findings.

Boss. Will you be doing this on company time?

Assistant. I will, but it should take no more than an hour, and I think we'll find that the benefits of the program will far exceed that one-hour investment.

Boss. All right, go ahead. But don't do anything without telling me first.

Investigate—Level 2

At the next stage, the boss is not yet certain of the extent to which he can trust the assistant to do her job first and an improvement project second. (Note that he mentions a report being submitted on time.)

Assistant. Thank you, Jerry, for taking the time to meet with me today. I won't need more than a few minutes to outline a proposal to you—a proposal for a series of lunchtime lectures.

Boss. I don't have time to get involved with that.

Assistant. You won't have to get involved. You'll only need to make one choice out of three I present to you. Let me explain. R. Competitor is having a successful series of lunchtime lectures. I think our employees could benefit from a comparable program. I'd like to investigate the possibility of having some professors at the local college address our staff members during lunch.

Boss. What's it going to cost?

Assistant. That's one of the things I have to investigate. I'll make a few calls and send you a memo with my recommendations.

Boss. Fine, just make sure you finish the Bixby report by noon today.

Assistant. You'll have it on your desk by eleven.

Boss. Great—and by the way, I appreciate your taking the time to help the company in our learning efforts.

As trust grows, so will the degree of empowerment. As the assistant advances up the ladder of empowerment, she will find more and more opportunities to demonstrate her value to the organization.

Intend—Level 3

The assistant at this level takes some initiative but does not make any permanent commitments.

> ASSISTANT. Thank you, Jeannette, for taking the time to meet with me today. I've done an informal survey of our staff and have found there is considerable interest in a series of lunchtime lectures. I was surprised at how responsive people were, so I went ahead and made some tentative arrangements.
>
> BOSS. What kind of arrangements?
>
> ASSISTANT. Just two, really. I found that the conference room is available next Thursday so we would have a place to meet. And then I learned that a local consultant is willing to conduct a demonstration lecture for one hour on the topic of time management.
>
> BOSS. What's it going to cost?
>
> ASSISTANT. Surprise! There is no cost—at least not for this lecture. If we want the consultant to return and do a full-day seminar, *then* there will be a cost.
>
> BOSS. What happens after this first lecture?
>
> ASSISTANT. I want to evaluate how well it works. If the response is positive, I'd like to contact other consultants in the area to see if they'd be willing to do the same thing.
>
> BOSS. Well, proceed then. You said the topic for Thursday is time management? Maybe I'll drop by myself.

The assistant feels confident that her boss will have no problem with her initial overtures but has not finalized any arrangements until she obtains her approval.

Inform—Level 4

Notice the subtle shifts occurring in the relationship between the boss and the assistant

> ASSISTANT. Thank you, Jerry, for taking the time to meet with me today. I wanted to give you an update on a project I started a few weeks back. You may remember my mentioning I wanted to have a few meetings with employees at lunchtime, with one of them teaching the rest of us a particular skill.

Boss. Right. How's it going?

Assistant. It's been getting better each time. For the first meeting, Sue spoke about global market developments. We had only five people there, but we really learned a lot. By the time of the second meeting, thirteen people had signed up to hear Tim discuss enterprise database access. He even had handouts for us. For the next meeting, we have twenty-four people signed up, and we're running out of space in the conference room.

Boss. Hmmm. Let me give Sam a call. He owes me one, and maybe I can persuade him to give up that fancy coffee room for just one day. When do you want it?

Assistant. We're scheduled for next Thursday.

Boss. Okay. I'll get back to you on this.

Assistant. Thanks. By the way, you may want to come to the next one. We have a new call center automation vendor coming in, and I know you are particularly interested in improving our efficiency in this area.

Boss. I'll be there!

There is greater collegiality at this level, with the two functioning almost as partners, as true co-workers. In fact, the boss is going out of his way to strengthen the assistant's program by trying to get another room for the meeting. Further, he is going to report back to the assistant on availability, rather than the other way around. As the exchange ends, we find the two sharing information, assisting each other on both the personal and professional levels.

Independent—Level 5

Clearly, at the *in*dependent level of operation, the boss has complete confidence in the assistant's abilities.

> ASSISTANT. I'm glad you asked about those lunchtime lectures, Jeannette. I've been meaning to let you know how well they went. This week's session had eighty-six people in attendance.
>
> BOSS. Wow! What's your secret?
>
> ASSISTANT. No secret really. I found a good formula and stuck with it. First, we do a needs assessment to learn the topics employees are interested in . Then we find a volunteer speaker and have the person do a trial run to be sure the lecture won't be boring. And then we send out e-mail notices and wait for people to show up.
>
> BOSS. What else are you thinking of doing?
>
> ASSISTANT. Actually, I've been thinking of turning the whole project over to Mike. He's really good at organizing things like this, and I'd like to move on to a new project.
>
> BOSS. What do you have in mind?
>
> ASSISTANT. Well, I've been thinking about a benchmarking project or else assembling a customer focus group.
>
> BOSS. They both sound worthwhile. Let me know if there's anything I can do to assist.

Boss and assistant have probably been working together for quite a while. The boss trusts her assistant enough to know that her projects will benefit the organization and does not have to function in a micromanagerial function.

Handling Difficult Situations

The dialogues presented as illustrations of the 5-*In* Model reflect ideal circumstances. However, it is not an ideal world. In the real world, when human beings come in contact with one another, problems arise and conflicts erupt. There is much that can be done, however, to prevent difficult situations from ever developing, or if they do develop, to prevent them from escalating to explosive hostilities.

You can display sensitivity to others in any number of ways. When you realize how vulnerable most people are, how fragile the psyche really is, how many people lack self-confidence, then you can begin to think about your own actions and how they might be regarded an uncaring or unkind. Often without ever intending to cause pain, we do so—by a careless remark, an unguarded facial expression, a thoughtless gesture.

Before you speak, think about how your words may affect your listeners. Before you interrupt, realize that such an action is a sign of dismissal (you didn't think the other person's ideas were worth listening to in their entirety). As former (now impeached) Arizona governor Evan Meacham once observed, "If I had to do it all over again, I would realize that style is as important as substance."

With the Boss

Difficult situations usually center on one of two sets of circumstances: You have negative information about the boss, or she has negative information about you. In the former case, you may hear—and agree with—some less-than-flattering comments made about her. Or you may feel that there are areas in which she could easily do better. In either case, you owe it to the boss and the company to share information that will help her improve. If, for example, her time management skills are virtually nonexistent, you could tell her about an upcoming seminar on the topic.

Of course, if she is the kind of person who may fire you for daring to offer critical comments, let someone else provide this information. But if the two of you have a fairly good relationship and you are confident of your diplomatic skills, plan your strategy and then proceed. The following checklist will be useful for most situations in which you are offering less-than-positive feedback to your boss:

☐ *Assess the circumstances.* If your boss solicits your opinion, you can be direct—but be delicate too. If she has not asked for feedback but you feel she needs to have it, you will have to find a way to supply it—directly or indirectly. The direct way is to share your perceptions or knowledge. Depending, of course, on the degree of rapport you have with her, you might say something like, "In the staff meeting the other day, I noticed that a few of the employees were having trouble following the slides you had prepared. I took a public speaking course a few years ago and I remember the instructor insisting, 'Never have more than three points on a slide.' If you like, I can look over your slides for the next presentation and quickly fix those that may be overloaded with data." The indirect way would be to leave a relevant article on her desk with a note saying, "Knowing that you're always interested in ways to improve in this area, I thought you'd enjoy reading this."

☐ *Have specific examples ready.* True, you don't want to talk down to your boss or be so blunt as to say, "Your presentation didn't really introduce us to the main points and at the end, there was no summary" (although that may be the case), but you should be specific. Say something like, "The only thing I found missing was an introduction of the main points and a summary. Then it would have been outstanding."

☐ *Do not overwhelm.* Rather than present a laundry list of everything that needs improvement, select the one or two most serious problems, and concentrate on those.

☐ *Check to see if your points are getting across.* If your boss is showing signs of impatience or is speaking in "closed" body language, fashion a gracious verbal exit. For example, "We can discuss this more fully at a later time if you like," or "I've covered quite a bit here. Why don't I stop, and if you want to discuss any of this later, just give me a call."

☐ *Plan a strategy.* If the boss has agreed with some or all of your observations, offer to assist. Devise a plan that will benefit the boss when similar circumstances present themselves.

In the second situation, your boss may be privy to criticisms of your behavior, or she may have made her own assessments regarding areas in which you may need improvement. When you are the recipient of observations that may be less than positive, follow these guidelines:

☐ *Listen nondefensively.* The boss may be incorrect or inaccurate about the observations she is sharing, but—right or wrong—they are still her perceptions. Rather than deny or contradict them, try to find out what caused her to hold those impressions of you.

☐ *If you have a fairly good idea in advance of what the meeting will entail, come prepared.* To illustrate, if you know the boss has received a complaint about your work, have a succinct explanation ready and also an outline of what you will do to ensure the problem doesn't happen again.

☐ *If you find yourself becoming emotional, try a "trick" or postpone the rest of the meeting.* One of the most-favored tricks for people who find themselves becoming tearful is to press their tongue as hard as possible against the roof of their mouth. Another is to acknowledge mentally that the meeting is very difficult but that it is nothing in comparison to the difficulties of someone you know, who suffers from a serious illness or has experienced a terrible loss. If neither trick works and you find yourself overcome with emotion, simply say, "I prefer to discuss this at another time," and leave the room.

☐ *Ask for assistance.* Whether the "bad news" concerns the loss of a job, pay raise, or promotion, or simply the need for improvement, ask the boss for ways to improve the situation in the future.

With Coworkers

As surely as the sun rises each morning, there will be run-ins with coworkers. The important thing to remember is that these conflicts can be resolved no matter how divisive they may initially seem. All it takes is the right attitude. (Remember, if for no other reason than your own good health, it is important not to let negative feelings linger.)

☐ *Watch body language.* It will tell you if the person is getting angry (you need to become more conciliatory), if the person is agreeing with you (you can elaborate on your points), or if the person has tuned you out (you need to catch his attention or else hold the discussion at a later time).

□ *If you anticipate the session will be difficult, have a neutral third party present.* Choose someone you both trust and respect who can listen to both of you as you give and take feedback and can ensure the exchange is kept under control.

□ *Admit the part you played in making the situation problematic.* Something you said or did has caused the other person to experience conflict. Elicit input about your behavior and then offer the same to the other person.

□ *End the meeting on a positive note.* Each of you should have been willing to make some concession so that your future dealings will be better than the present ones. Agree to meet again so progress can be assessed.

With Customers

Whether or not you are officially designated as a customer service representative, you always have customers—internal or external. Sometimes you will be caught off-guard by a customer's complaint. Nonetheless, with sufficient pratice, the following actions will become second nature to you. When they do, you will find yourself able to maintain composure no matter how difficult the circumstances:

□ *Take notes.* Your customer will see that you are taking the matter seriously. Notes will also provide you with accurate information as you follow through on the complaint.

□ *Reassure the customer.* If your response to the customer's complaint is, "Oh, that happens all the time," the customer is bound to lose faith, and you are bound to lose a customer. Instead, offer a reassuring statement such as, "I'm very sorry to hear that. It really is not typical of our policy." Additionally, gratitude *should* be the reaction, yet so often annoyance is the response the customer receives.

□ *Do not interrupt.* Rather, list questions or your note pad, but wait until the appropriate time to ask them. When a customer feels she needs to vent, it is best to allow venting to occur unabated.

☐ *Explain what will be done, if not by you then by someone else.* The customer has taken time to bring a problem to your attention. Tell what steps you and the company will follow to prevent such occurrences in the future. Assure the customer the complaint will be handled efficiently by detailing what you are going to do.

Developing a Can-Do Attitude

Attitude, they say, is more important than aptitude. The most skillful secretary in the world will not last long if she has an attitude problem. You need to get motivated and project the all-important can-do attitude.

A recent survey of 1,600 employees by Response Analysis of Princeton, New Jersey, found three factors of paramount importance in motivating workers to go beyond what is expected of them. As you read them, you will probably nod your head in agreement:

1. Giving an employee responsibility for her own work but also for the results achieved

2. Acknowledging the worth of an employee's effort

3. Aligning tasks to the skills of the employee

You can stop nodding now and begin making notes in response to these questions:

1. How can you achieve a greater degree of autonomy over the work and the results expected of you? _____

_____

_____

2. How can you gain more recognition for your excellence? How can you ensure that others receive the recognition they deserve?

_____

_____

3. When is the last time you sat down with your boss to discuss what you believe are the greatest contributions you can make to the organization? _____

_____

_____

Here are more questions for you:

Within the last six months...	Yes	No
1. I have volunteered to do a job no one else wanted to do.	____	____
2. I have formed a team to work on an improvement project.	____	____
3. I have attended a workshop or seminar.	____	____
4. I have offered to be a mentor for someone.	____	____
5. I have written an article for the company newsletter or an outside journal.	____	____
6. I have benchmarked (compared work processes) with other assistants.	____	____
7. I have attended a meeting sponsored by a professional organization.	____	____
8. I have made my boss aware of a new skill I have acquired.	____	____
9. I have read a book or article about my profession.	____	____
10. I have made a suggestion to my boss for improving some aspect of the job.	____	____

If the majority of your answers were in the yes column, your attitude is probably already can-do—in which case you should begin thinking about ways to help others acquire a similar attitude. If the majority of your answers appear in the no column, undertake some of the suggestions implied in the questions in order to convert "don't-do" to "can-do" and "will-do" actions.

Assuming Leadership

The preceding questions contain the seeds of leadership actions. But what sort of person is willing to nurture those seeds to fruition? As you read about some of the traits commonly associated with leadership, ask yourself if the descriptions could apply to you:

☐ *Energetic.* **Leaders bring a strong sense of purpose to their work. Their enthusiasm is apparent in the way they attack the projects before them. Their unbridled fervor is usually not hampered by hurdles or setbacks. Leaders who have energy for their tasks usually manage to energize others as well.**

How energetic are you? How energetic do others think you are?

☐ *Self-confident.* **Leaders view themselves in a positive light, unabashedly admitting what they can do well and determined to use their talents to effect positive change. After all, if leaders do not have faith in themselves, how can they expect their followers to? Leaders are honest but not conceited about their ability. They are willing to experiment and able to maintain movement toward a goal, certain that it will ultimately be reached.**

How confident are you? How confident do others think you are?

☐ *Motivational.* **Leaders believe in what they are doing. They are caught up in the energy generated by pursuing a project in which they are deeply interested. They are enamored of the work they do. When real estate developer Trammel Crow, for example, was asked the secret of his success, he replied, "Love." We do best what we love doing, and the leader's enthusiasm invariably spills over and magnetizes the interest of those who follow her lead.**

Are you motivated enough by your work to initiate improvements? How willing are others to follow your lead?

☐ *Ethical.* We rightfully expect that our leaders will demonstrate a high ethical sense, be honest in their dealings, and exhibit honor and trustworthiness as they interact with others. Leaders have a sense of social responsibility, and are concerned with improving the quality of (work) life for many people—not just themselves. Numerous studies underscore the importance of integrity as a success component.

How ethical are you? How ethical do others think you are?

☐ *Growth-oriented.* Leaders learn as much as they can—not only about the issues that consume them but also about themselves and others. They learn to improve their own image by studying the successful traits of admirable others and then incorporating these traits into their own behaviors. They also concern themselves with the growth of others, believing that elevating the status of all benefits all.

How have you grown in the last six months? Are others aware of your improvement efforts?

Tips From Lucy A. Mastri
Eastman Kodak Company

KNOWLEDGE

- Know the goals, mission, and expectations of your manager and your entire organization. Make these goals your own.

- Develop resources of key people who can help put out fires.

- Know the facts before you act.

ACCOUNTABILITY

- Get a reputation for reliability by saying what you will do and then doing what you say you will do. This is my personal number 1 priority.

- Be ethical, and stick to your values.

- Think first. Then communicate your ideas.

MOTIVATION

- Be self-directed. Anticipate needs before they become needs.

- Do more than is expected. You will be perceived as managerial.

- See the forest, not the trees.

- Learn to shift gears as needed.

- Think win-win.

COMMITMENT

- Be willing to do the unpleasant.

- Be a decision maker, even on small items.

- Don't drop the ball. Follow up to get results.

Tips From Sabina C. Borchers
Eastman Kodak Company

CONFIDENCE

- Know your job and know the people with whom you have daily contact; this affects the way you communicate with them.

- Trust yourself and your judgment when making decisions.

ATTITUDE

- Have confidence in yourself. This automatically brings forth a positive attitude. Confidence is demonstrated in verbal communications as well as in your body language.

- Remember Confucius's words, "Find work you love to do and you will never have to work for the rest of your life."

INITIATIVE

- Project in advance the needs for upcoming meetings or projects. This is something all self-starters do.

- Share new ideas and goals with supervisors.

- Show initiative by having a "just-do-it" approach.

Tips From Wendy A. Young
Eastman Kodak Company

- Demonstrate a winning attitude, pride, and self-confidence. They lead to superior performance. People who demonstrate these characteristics will be encouraged and supported.

- Become a manager within your own area of responsibility.

- Take a global, rather than task-oriented, approach to each day's activities.

- Have a thorough knowledge of your organization.

- Develop a high commitment to the value of giving and receiving feedback for continually improving team and individual effectiveness.

- Be willing to get involved and work with others to get things done correctly. Such actions will develop your leadership characteristics.

- Encourage yourself and others to establish an organizational culture that invites participation and involvement. These actions lead to understanding, commitment, and contribution, which result in sound relationships and better rapport.

- Throughout the organization, build relationships founded on trust and respect.

- Show anticipation and preparation. They are key elements of leaders, not followers.

- Keep a healthy balance between being assertive and being receptive. Being able to move along the continuum will make you more skillful in handling various work situations.

- Build a network. When you invest your time and energy in others, they become valuable allies when you need support.

- Observe your boss's natural pace of work, and adjust your methods accordingly.

- Look and feel like a success—every day.

- Remind yourself periodically that ability will never catch up with the demand for it.

2

Organizing the Work

Analyzing Tasks

If you enjoy analyzing large projects in order to determine the most efficient way to manage them, you possess a significant skill, and may also be creating a positive mind-set without even realizing it. Psychologists at the University of Virginia have found that employees who work intensively at a project requiring analysis and organization raise their spirits without even attempting to do so. The researchers showed depressing movies to 112 people. Afterward, those who worked actively and deeply on given assignments reported feeling more cheerful than those who were only mildly engaged. Work that requires you to stretch your mind, but not to the point of anxiety, is the best kind of work for chasing the blues away.

The secret to handling large projects facing you is to divide them into a series of small projects, each with its own deadline. The following case study is based on an actual boss, who is always in a hurry, and his dutiful assistant, who prides herself on being able to second-guess his articulated, half-articulated, and unarticulated intents. As you put yourself in her shoes, decide what you would do before, during, and especially after his instructions have been given.

> *[The date is Tuesday, January 25. N. Aheree, founder of a small publishing firm, is rushing out the door, late for a meeting with the executive council. He pauses long enough to catch his breath so that he can exhale these directions to his secretary, Effie Shunt.]*
>
> N. AHEREE *[spoken very quickly].* By Friday, we need to send off the chapters to all the contributors, asking them to return them with any corrections by mid-February. When the chapters are returned, incorporate the changes into the manuscript, and have the whole thing ready by the end of February. Contact Tim and tell him we need that foreword asap. Go through the permissions folder and be sure permission letters have been sent to each contributor. You need to proofread all the chapters, of course, and do an index, and contact the artist. We've got to have those illustrations back by mid-February. The printer needs the final manuscript by March 1 if we're going to meet the production schedule. Any questions?
>
> Ms. SHUNT *[with a touch of smugness].* Of course not!
>
> N. AHEREE *[as he exits].* Gosh! What would I do without you?
>
> Ms. SHUNT *[sotto voice].* Probably lose your job.
>
> N. AHEREE. Oh, one more thing. Please make reservations at Perrino's for noon. Today's the day I interview the movie star.

Where to begin? Let's look at the pretorrent flood. If you had worked for Mr. Aheree for more than a day, you would be familiar with his style, in which case, you would have paper and pen *always* ready. Better yet, you would have a tape recorder wound and ready to record his directions and directives, invariably delivered with machine-gun rapidity. If you were truly interested in avoiding the stress involved with scenarios like this one, you would try to meet with him at the beginning of each day in order to learn his priorities. Admittedly, this is not always possible. Nor is it likely that his day will always go as planned. Nonetheless, having a routine whereby each of you is kept informed of the other's priorities will make the day go much more smoothly.

Ms. Shunt prides herself on her listening skills and her ability to think as her boss thinks. She is loathe to ask questions, believing they convey a lack of efficiency. However, it is better to get clarity beforehand than to get chastised afterward. If you have worked with your boss for a very long time, you probably *do* know how he wants things done, and if the project is one you have done several times before, you will have a minimum of questions. Still, it's better to ask if you are unsure than to make mistakes you will later regret.

In one long paragraph and a ten-word addendum in the case study is enough work to keep the secretary busy for the next several weeks. To organize the many priorities, a chart will prove most useful:

Attend to Immediately	**Attend to by These Dates**
_____	_____
_____	_____
_____	_____
_____	_____

Given this simple division, which of the tasks from Mr. Aheree would you put in which column? (You'll find the answers at the end of the chapter.)

Another simple model can be employed to help you organize the many projects that constitute your job:

1. Begin by making a list of all the unfinished work you have to do in relation to your job. Include things you must do, want to do, and should do. Don't overlook tasks that are ongoing, tasks you have already started, tasks that you need not begin for awhile. In other words, look at the totality of your job with the eye of an outsider. One way to do this is to assume you have won a six-month world cruise and you are leaving instructions for the person who will handle your work during that period.

2. Divide the items on the list into categories (e.g., teamwork, continuous learning, general office management). Be sure each item fits into a category.

3. Transfer each category to a page of its own, leaving room at the top for pertinent information. Record whatever information is important for your own purposes. Typically that information includes:

- The current date
- The date by which you hope to have all the items on the page completed
- The "customer" or person to whom a project will be delivered
- Names of those who should be included or consulted
- Any other pertinent information

4. Organize the category-pages in prioritized fashion. Then prioritize the items within each category.

Developing Teamwork

Teams composed of diverse individuals, research shows, are more productive than teams that are homogeneous in every regard.

The richness inherent in diversity stems from the differences and the appreciation of those differences. Think of all the ways you differ from those who might serve on a team with you. There are gender differences, educational differences, socioeconomic differences, and cultural, racial, and ethnic differences. There are age differences, experiential differences, and differences in the talents we bring to the table.

Further, the ways in which each of us processes information are different, as are our problem-solving and decision-making styles—to say nothing of the differences in our traditions, values, and attitudes. When we have a group of people who think, act, and believe in exactly the same way, we have a group headed for trouble. For example, one trouble spot for teams with a collective mind-set is the danger of groupthink—that is, the desire to be part of the group is so strong that individuals hesitate to offer differing points of view. There are other trouble spots too—for example, the tendency to approach problems from a singular perspective or the inclination to view data within anticipated parameters rather than search for additional data or pursue unusual trends.

When you are joining a team for the first time, make certain you (as leader or as team member) arrange to have some time spent on understanding and developing respect for the diversity within the group. One way is to ask each person to answer, in round-robin fashion, a question based on some of the differences cited earlier—for example, "What experiences have you had that might be useful to our team as we work on this project?" or "What special talents do you have that you'd like to use as our team pursues its mission?"

There is a multiplicative power that teams enjoy: the energy that is released from their collective efforts. Teams, especially when they meet success with the early projects, are energized to tackle projects of increasing difficulty. If initial projects fail, however, team members may be so discouraged that they refrain from joining another team for awhile.

Here is a list of characteristics common to high-performance teams. Compare these descriptions to the team on which you currently serve (or the next one you join).

Characteristics of High-Performance Teams

- Membership is limited to six to eight members.

- Members accept the natural evolution of teams (first described by Bruce Tuckman): Form—Storm—Norm—Perform. When teams initially come together, they are in the *form* stage, which is characterized by uncertainty and apprehension. These feelings lead to the *storms* that erupt in the second stage as team members begin to wrestle with issues like hidden agendas or power struggles. In time, under strong leadership, the teams begin to *norm*, to establish the ground rules by which the members agree to abide. It is at this stage that the mission takes precedence over individual desires. Not until teams have gone through the first three stages can they *perform* effectively.

- At least one member is knowledgeable, one is practical, and one is creative.

- The members answer "I do!" to one or both of these questions: "Who knows?" "Who cares?"

- They have established ground rules.

- Agendas are used for all meetings.

- The members assess their own progress.

- Someone champions their cause.

- Their mission is challenging but not impossible.

- Members are prepared for possible rejection—in the form of a denial of their request for additional funds, or as criticism from an approving authority. Or it may be that their proposal is not accepted.

- The team can make an excellent presentation to the senior management.

Establishing Partnerships

Due in large measure to the influence of the quality movement, today's work environment bears little resemblance to what used to be. The business of running a business is changing—almost daily, it sometimes seems. New partnerships are being formed, new communication tools are being employed, new structures are being established. Leadership itself has undergone change, resulting in influence, according to author Masaaki Imai, based on "personal experience and conviction and not necessarily on authority, rank, or age."

The democratization of leadership has created an exhilarating freedom for employees, who are in environments that value empowerment. When individuals and teams are acknowledged for the experience, conviction, and intelligence they possess and when the organization willingly uses the talents of employees eager to share, then everyone benefits.

New structures are being formed in organizations—structures that include people who in the past may not have interacted with one another, even though they worked at various stages of the same process: union representatives working on teams with managers, for example, or secretaries working on teams with bosses. We see, in short, a new spirit of respect, cooperation, and a willingness to work together.

Because partnerships are established on the basis of mutual benefit, consider both what you can give and what you can get as far as a partnership project is concerned. As you consider possibilities for partnering, use the "big-picture" perspective rather than the "piece-of-the-puzzle" perspective. Bosses are always good choices for partners, but so are other employees within the organization; other secretaries in other companies, even in other states or countries; educational institutions; community agencies; nonprofit organizations. The list is unending.

> A good example of partnering can be found in the Mount Carmel Medical Center ASSET group (Administrative Support/Secretarial Enrichment Team) in Columbus, Ohio, which joined forces (and split costs) with the Eagles team (Empowered Action Group Leading and Excelling in Support) of the Franciscan Health System in Cincinnati to share a keynote speaker for their April secretarial conferences. The speaker agreed to drive between the cities, thus eliminating the need for two separate plane fares. Both organizations profited from the arrangement, as did the speaker, who was able to arrange two speaking engagements on subsequent days.
>
> Another example is the secretary who arranged for a local law enforcement officer to address a group of employees regarding safety issues. The police benefited from the publicity and, more important, from the very real possibility that the officer's remarks would help decrease the incidence of crime. The audience benefited from his remarks. And the secretary who initiated the partnership benefited from the increased visibility and self-confidence that she derived as a result of her work.

Here are the steps to establishing a work-related partnership.

1. Identify an important work-related issue on which you would like to be better informed and to which you believe you can make a valuable contribution.

2. Think of some person, unit, team, agency, organization, or institution with whom you would like to partner.

3. Approach the other person or entity with a proposal detailing expectations, benefits, and the extent of time, money, and work each party will need to provide.

4. Establish a series of meetings (electronic, telephonic, personal), and adhere to the schedule until the project has been completed or the partnership terminated.

Solving Problems Effectively

To which of these views on problem solving do you gravitate the most?

Mark Twain:	"Even if you are on the right track, you'll get run over if you stand there long enough."
Roger Dawson:	"If Edison had been a CEO of a conglomerate, he probably would have insisted upon the invention of the world's best oil lantern instead of inventing the lightbulb."
Cicero:	"Any man may make a mistake; none but a fool will persist in it."
Picasso:	"Computers are useless; they only give you answers."
Jonas Salk:	"Intuition is my partner. I wake up every morning to see what gifts it will toss me."
Henry Ford:	(responding to an efficiency expert's complaint about a daydreaming employee): "That man once had an idea that saved us millions of dollars. At the time, I believe his feet were planted right where they are now."

Thomas Edison:	"I'm experimenting upon an instrument that does for the eye what the phonograph does for the ear [the motion picture projector]."
Herman Melville:	"After all, a smooth sea never made a successful sailor."
Sun Tzu:	"Opportunities multiply if they are seized."
Henry Kaiser:	"A problem is an opportunity in work clothes."
Cicero:	"The greater the difficulty, the greater the glory."
Robert Schuller:	"Problems are not stop ssigns, they are guidelines."
Arthur Schopenhauer:	"To overcome difficulties is to experience the full delight of existence."
J. C. Penney:	"I am grateful for all my problems. After each one was overcome, I became stronger and more able to meet those that were still to come. I grew in all my difficulties."
Linus (Peanuts):	"There is no problem too big we can't run away from."
Robert Frost:	"The brain is a wonderful organ; it starts working the moment you get up in the morning and does not stop until you get into the office."

Which did you select, and why? _____

_____

Analyze your basic response to the existence of problems. This simple quiz may assist.

	True	False
1. I believe some good comes from all the obstacles life places in our path.	____	____
2. I welcome challenges.	____	____

	True	False
3. I tend to believe things happen for a reason.	____	____
4. As I look over my life, I realize I have never faced a hurdle that I could not overcome with some degree of success.	____	____
5. I am grateful for the blessings I have been given.	____	____

If you honestly introspect and can truly answer at least three of these questions in the affirmative, you are probably approaching life with a realistic yet optimistic perspective. If you had three or more "false" answers, though, your attitude most likely needs adjustment.

What kind of attitude (toward the existence of problems) do you admire in others? _____

_____

How difficult would it be for you to emulate this kind of thinking?

_____

Who could assist as you set about making these adjustments?

_____

Problems, according to U.S. industrialist Henry Kaiser, are "opportunities in work clothes." Keep that in mind along with this dictum: "Never go to your boss with just a problem. Go with a problem *and* three possible solutions." In other words, the problem itself is an opportunity to demonstrate to your boss:

- Your initiative

- Your creativity

- Your willingness to work in partnership with her

- Your awareness of her busy schedule and so your reluctance to dump more problems on it

- Your desire to be empowered enough to work on the problem's solution

How do you come up with solutions? you may be wondering. Brainstorming, of course, will generate many potentially workable solutions. There are additional approaches, however, that you may not yet have tried.

Janusian Thinking

Janus was the Roman god after whom the month of January was named. On ancient coins, he is shown in profile, facing in two different directions—looking back over the year that has just ended and looking forward to the year that is about to begin. When we think in Janusian terms, we think about opposites.

Reversals of thought can lead to very exciting and successful outcomes. To illustrate, every mystery story you have ever read has probably had the identity of the killer revealed at the very end of the story. But the creators of the highly successful *Columbo* television series decided to do the opposite: They identified the killer within the first moments of each episode and then proceeded to show how that crafty Columbo was able to establish guilt.

Try to tackle your next problem with a Janusian approach. It won't work in every situation, but it will surely yield novel ideas for some of your problems.

Reification

If the reification technique were a movie, it would be *Field of Dreams*. The most famous line from that movie was, "If you build it, they will come." By extension, the reification method asserts that if you make a single move toward the solution of a problem, the reality of solution will follow in time.

Consider the problem of weight loss. It is easy to talk about how hard it is to lose weight. Much harder is *doing* something about it. But a single move in the right direction will lead to reification or the reality of solution. In this case, placing a phone call to Weight Watchers, or consulting a physician, or going on a diet with a friend leads to the ultimate desired outcome. The difficulty is making that single but significant first reifying step.

Force Field Analysis

Originated by psychologist Kurt Lewin, this user-friendly technique asks you to set out the current state or actual problem you are facing. Then you describe the ideal state or the perfect solution to this problem.

In the force field analysis, you identify the driving forces and the restraining forces that are affecting your ability to move from the current to the ideal:

Driving Forces	Restraining Forces
_____	_____
_____	_____
_____	_____
_____	_____
_____	_____

You can now determine how to maximize the driving forces and minimize the restraining forces.

360° Thinking

While the 360° method is more structured than simple brainstorming, it allows for wild speculation nonetheless. It takes you full circle, so to speak. The first 270 degrees (90-, 180-, 270-degree quadrants) encourage creativity, while the last 90-degree angle forces order upon your thoughts.

When you engage in this kind of thinking, you agree to work within a structured framework for a specific period of time. Decide in advance how long you or your team wish to spend on the idea-generation phase of problem solving. Let us say that you feel twenty minutes would be sufficient. You then regard that period of time as a pie, divided into four slices. The first three are four minutes each. The last is eight minutes (you need extra time at the end).

In the first quadrant, for four minutes, you silently record any thoughts that are in your mind—*any* thoughts, whether or not they relate to the problem at hand. For the next four minutes, you focus your thoughts on the actual problem, and list only ideas that could possibly solve the problem.

When you concentrate on the third four-minute segment, you list only wild, absurd, "nutty" ideas. Filter them as you think, and list only those that are truly zany. Your final quadrant, and final time slot, asks that you quickly review the three lists and make a final list of workable, practical ideas.

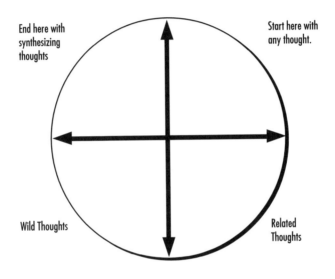

End here with
synthesizing
thoughts

Start here with
any thought.

Wild Thoughts

Related
Thoughts

A-S-K Approach

Subject an existing process, plan, or situation to three questions:

A *What can we Add?* More time? More color? More usage? More people? More research? More methods? More comparisons? More combinations? More practice? More options? More reasons? More parts? More ingredients?

S *What can we Subtract?* Should it be smaller, condensed, streamlined, divided, split? Should we modify, calibrate, refine, omit, revise? Should we distill, clean, polish, reorganize, replace?

K *What can we Knit?* Can we knit together the existing process with precedents? With emerging trends? With ideas from other fields? With other approaches? With other persons? Can we combine methods or purposes? Can we apply this to another situation or use? Can we exchange or interchange?

Making Good Decisions

Effective problem solving and effective decision making go hand in hand. It is clearly futile to brainstorm workable possibilities if poor decisions are then made about which possibility to pursue.

The following questions will help you define and then refine your strategy for making good decisions. Spend time with them over the next week or so, and discuss them with friends and coworkers:

Ask Questions

How many decisions do you make a day? What types of decisions are they? _____

_____

_____

What is an example of a meaningful decision you have recently made? _____

_____

_____

What process do you use in making decisions? _____

_____

_____

Does the process differ when you make decisions about family? Finance? Career? _____

_____

_____

Do you seek the opinions of others? Under what circumstances?

_____

_____

_____

Do you use the opinions of others? How? _____

_____

_____

How often are the decisions you make the right ones? _____

_____

_____

What clouds the efficiency or excellence of your decisions? _____

_____

_____

Do you typically reduce the decision to an either-or choice? _____

_____

_____

How do you know when you have made the right decisions?_____

_____

_____

How is "rightness" determined? _____

_____

_____

What are the three most important decisions you have made in your life? _____

_____

_____

How would your life have been different if you had made other choices? _____

_____

_____

Do your least important decisions take the least amount of time?

_____

_____

_____

Use Your Intuition—*If* You Are Intuitive

It is altogether possible that you are an intuitive decision maker. Some people are and are quite successful with this style. They should continue with it. Others use the "gut decision" style but have not assessed the worth of the results. Nonetheless, they continue with this style, not knowing if a more analytical style would be preferable. The best way to assess the value of decisions you make on the visceral level is to keep a log.

For every decision you make over a week, record the type of decision you made: **I** for intuitive decisions and **W** for well researched. As soon as you are able to assess the results of your decision, record your degree of satisfaction with the outcome, using a scale of 1 to 5, with 5 representing a decision with which you are quite pleased. At the end of the week, review those high-score decisions. If the majority of them were **I** decisions, you are using the "golden gut." If your **I** decisions received low scores, however, you should reconsider your dependency on this type of decision making.

There is a simple way to gauge the accuracy of decisions made because a particular choice simply feels right. Answer a set of questions, such as those that follow. Don't overanalyze the choices; merely respond as quickly as you can to the answer that you are drawn to.

1. *Younker* is

   (a) a small sea fish.

   (b) turkey stuffing.

   (c) a young man.

   (d) a know-it-all.

2. **Sternutation** is

   (a) the act of sneezing.

   (b) a mixture of sand and gravel.

   (c) strong, unglazed cotton.

   (d) a cardiovascular procedure.

3. **Philagrypnia** means

   (a) needing to be in the presence of other people.

   (b) having a tendency toward criminal behavior.

   (c) a husband's faked illness.

   (d) needing less sleep than most other people.

4. **Ruction** is

   (a) a tooth extraction.

   (b) a noisy quarrel.

   (c) life on a farm.

   (d) a road along a mountain cliff.

5. **Huckle** means

   (a) a hip or haunch.

   (b) a type of edible mushroom.

   (c) a lizard.

   (d) a fever accompanied by chills.

(Answers appear at the end of this chapter.)

Apply the D-E-C-I-D-E Technique

You'll find the D-E-C-I-D-E technique useful in analyzing and ameliorating your decision-making style:

Describe the decisions to be made.

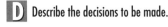 Elicit the input of those whose decision-making ability you respect.

 Consider the assumptions surrounding the decisions to be made.

 Invest some time in asking questions and doing research on the situation.

Decide in advance what the consequences might be. How would you handle them? What about the reversibility of the decision?

Educate yourself about your style. Keep a log showing which decisions were least successful/most successful and why.

Answers to the Exercise on Page 25

The things that should be done immediately are:

Calling the restaurant for reservations. Because this involves an important person, because it could cause difficulty or embarassment for your boss if not attended to immediately, and because it just takes moments to do, it should be attended to right away.

Calling the artist. This can be done quickly and should be done immediately—given the length of time it takes an artist to create publishable images. Items like this, if they fall through the cracks, can shake the very foundation of a project.

Checking to see who has not yet returned the permission form. Another form can be sent out, as needed, when the chapters are sent to the contributors.

Calling Tim to request the foreword. A simple reminder call will require very little time, but if "ducks" like these are not lined up in a row, serious consequences could ensue.

The remaining tasks should be attended to in approximately this order:

By Friday, January 28, send out the chapters to all contributors. Include permission forms for those who have not already returned them.

On February 7, call and remind them that the chapters must be returned by February 15.

Between February 16 and 18, incorporate all changes made by contributors.

Between February 21 and 23, work on the index. (Think about this logically: there is no point in doing the index until all the changes have been made by the contributors and incorporated into the manuscript.)

On February 24 and 25, do the final proofreading. (This should not be done until the index is completed so it can also be given a final proofreading.)

On February 28, send the completed manuscript to the printer.

Answers to the Exercise on Pages 38 and 39

1.   (c)   2.   (a)   3. (d)   4.   (b)   5.   (a)

If you had three or more correct answers, you are probably one of the rare few who has the famed golden gut. To make certain that your correct answers were not simply lucky guesses, track your decisions for a week.

Tips From Beth Hood
Administrative Coordinator for the Executive
Office, Lockheed Martin Corporation

- Use an electronic database to track incoming correspondence, employing different fields to log information. When you receive inquiries, it's easy to pull up records on the computer screen and check to see what the disposition of the correspondence is.

- Organize daily schedules with an electronic calendar. There are many software packages available to suit individual needs. When preparing new schedules, never throw the old ones away. It's easy to omit important items inadvertently when updating. If you save the old ones, you can go back and check anything you've added.

- Set up predefined macros in your word processing package to fit each type of stationery your office uses. That way, it takes less time to set up correspondence before you begin typing.

- I use the Lotus Organizer to enter business addresses into an electronic database. Then I print them on peel-off labels and stick them on Rolodex cards. They are easily updated when changes occur and always look neat and clean because there are no scratch marks through the old information in the Rolodex.

- Use a shorthand pad to list every kind of note, inquiry, or action item that comes into the office, separating each item by a horizontal line. When each item has been completed, draw a diagonal line through it.

- An expanding day file is ideal for daily follow-up and action items. Organize upcoming events by month. At the end of a month, file the events you have accumulated chronologically in the daily follow-up file so that you are continually replacing old events with new ones.

- Keep an extra chronological copy of all outgoing correspondence without any attachments. That way, you can easily locate previous correspondence when you're not sure where you've filed something.

- Use half-sheets of 8 1/2-by 11-inch colored paper to type out telephone messages. Unlike the standardized small message pad sheets, they can easily be put in the follow-up file— and there's room to add any notes or action items. In addition, these sheets are not so easily lost.

- When you know your boss will be going on a trip, begin a trip file and accumulate information pertaining to it as you obtain it. By the time the trip date arrives, you will have all of the information you need.

- Create fax header sheets on the computer, and in a separate file save each new fax number you use. The numbers can be easily retrieved when you're rushing to send a fax. Only the date and number of pages will need to be changed. You can even add an automatic date code so that the date will change automatically each time you pull up the fax form.

3

Communicating

Using Persuasive Techniques

Author Vance Packard once defined leadership as "the art of getting others to want to do something that you are convinced should be done." Without a doubt, whenever we persuade others, we are actually leading them—ideally, in directions that will benefit them and the organization.

The persuaders who influence us most leave an impression worth recalling. That impression is created by words that are specific and succinct. The opposite of persuasive language is language that is ambiguous and misleading. Can you fathom what this 158-word sentence from an actual corporation's letter to stockholders means?

> In order to provide adequately for discretion in the Board of Directors of the Corporation with respect to providing non-contributory and contributory pension for employees under varying circumstances as occasion may require, it is considered necessary, as set forth in the attached plan for employee pension benefits, to continue the authority of the Board of Directors of the Corporation to authorize adoption of the pension provisions and benefits so as to provide different pension benefits of employee contributions from those set forth, to provide for the same or different benefits for other groups of employees, and to designate employees as being within or no longer within the coverage of any such pension benefits, all as the Board of Directors of the Corporation shall, in its discretion, from time to time believe to be required by the differing situations of various employees or groups of employees and in the best interests of the Corporation and its stockholders.

It's difficult to be persuaded when we don't understand what we're supposed to agree to. In addition to words that are specific and succinct, the most effective persuaders use words that are familiar and suitable for the occasion and for the audience.

Additional guidelines for persuasive communications include the following:

- Assess the situation. Then decide which approach will work best (typically a more assertive style when you have the upper hand, a more conciliatory style when you know you will encounter resistance).

- Anticipate objections, and be prepared to overcome them.

- Cite precedents whenever you can to strengthen your position.

- Do your homework. Have sufficient details at your fingertips so you can sound and be convincing.

- Ensure that the WIFM ("What's In it For Me?") factor is abundantly clear.

- Subordinate negative or unwelcome information by placing it carefully within the body of your argument. For example, if you are making a costly proposal, mention cost *after* you have listed benefits.

- Don't waste your reader's or listener's time with trivial or irrelevant data.

- Know what aspects of the corporate culture are important to the reader or listener (typically cost, speed, productivity) and emphasize those elements within the body of your persuasive appeal.

- Review the message to ensure there are no references that might be considered offensive.

- Ask others if they could or would endorse your plan so that when you present it, you can cite their approval.

- Show how your proposal supports the organization's mission.

- Seek a champion who can coach you through the stages of a persuasive presentation.

- If your proposal is denied, ask to implement it on a partial or pilot basis. Assure the boss that if it does not work during that time, you will abandon the effort. If it does work, you would like to expand and extend it.

Writing Letters and Memos in Just Five Minutes

Working in a do-more-with-less environment, you are undoubtedly overburdened, overworked, and underfunded. Yesterday you had one boss; today you may have two or even three. Consequently, you are always on the lookout for time-saving techniques. Here are some that will enable you to compose short memos and letters in just five minutes. The better you become at doing this, the more you will enjoy it, and the more you enjoy it, the more self-confidence you will acquire. Your composing competence may lead to more power as well, when your manager asks you to take on some of her writing tasks.

The PoDeUm Technique

This one (pronounced *podium*) is easy to remember and even easier to use. Here's how it works:

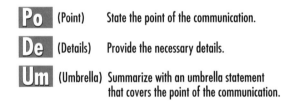

Po (Point)   State the point of the communication.

De (Details)   Provide the necessary details.

Um (Umbrella)   Summarize with an umbrella statement
                    that covers the point of the communication.

Let's say your boss has asked you to prepare a letter to the local university, declining an invitation to be the commencement speaker because she'll be out of town. Jotting down the needed elements, using the PoDeUm method, would quickly yield this outline:

 Po Boss is flattered but cannot accept

 De Will be out of town at conference

 Um Perhaps in future

Now that you have your outline, you can dash off a well-structured and professional communication. Just follow the outline prompted by the PoDeUm structure, and you'll find the words flowing from your frontal lobe to your fingertips.

> Dear Dean Onish:
>
> I am flattered to be invited as the commencement speaker for this year's exercises at Highland Community College. Unfortunately, I shall be out of town during that week, attending a professional conference in Ohio. Perhaps next year, we will be able to align our schedules so that I can accept an invitation from your fine school, from which many of our current employees have graduated.
>
> Thank you again for considering me.

Uncomplicated messages such as this can be organized in very little time. The PoDeUm method really works!

Free Association

This start-up method is like stream-of-consciousness writing, in that you begin writing whatever is on your mind at the moment. Your mind may wander into areas not related to the topic of your letter or memo, but keep on writing. Soon enough, your brain will redirect itself to the subject you should be concentrating on. The brain is never at a loss for words; it never stops thinking.

Within those recorded scrambled thoughts, you will find the genesis of your communication. Cross off anything that digresses and then use what remains to mold your communication.

Six-Word Starter

For some almost magical reason, by the time you have written these six words—"I want to tell you that"—the rest of the communication will virtually write itself. This beginning forces concentration on the gist of the message and unleashes a veritable torrent of necessary words.

Editing

Your communications reflect much about you. If you wish to be regarded as efficient and capable of assuming greater responsibility (which in time is recognized and rewarded), then your spoken and written messages must be efficient and accurate.

The writers of the following lines, taken from newspapers, no doubt spell-checked them. But as we all know, spell-check programs do not catch all errors.

> He had his girl fried with him on his trip south.

> He studied unclear physics at the Massachusetts Institute of Technology.

> In Chicago, six men have been accused of bride-taking.

> We have received a new shipment of shirts for men with 16 necks.

> The ambassador will visit the United States Nasal Academy.

I am not saying to avoid your spell-check program, just warning you to check a second time. Here are additional tips for finding errors of this nature:

- Scan the document quickly, and isolate the numbers. Then verify their accuracy. (A leading insurance company was once forced by the courts to pay $8 million because of a proofreading error.)

- Have a partner read your typed copy aloud while you listen and compare it to the original.

- Double-check your citations. If the text refers readers to page 42 in an appendix, turn to page 42 to see if the referenced page number is correct.

- Check for format consistency before beginning to read.

- If possible, put the document aside for a while, and come back to it later that day or even the next day. Proofread it again with a fresh, concentrated effort.

- Check dates against a calendar to be certain the dates are accurately listed. If the communication is typed in January, make certain you have the new year listed.

- If the original document was written with many inserts, number the paragraphs. Then go back after you have typed it, and check to see that your typed version has the same number of paragraphs that appeared in the fragmented original.

There are proofreading errors, and there are mechanical or grammatical errors. The errors in the following sentences are of the mechanical type. As such, they truly detract from the professionalism of the writer. Can you spot all eight of them?.

Each of us in the accounting offices look forward to meeting you and welcome you to our organization.

To maximize our efforts, the conference room will be reserved for the entire day.

The rationale being that an informal atmosphere is most conducive to analyzing the data, which is certain to be overwhelming.

We are anxious to discuss the following with you: monitoring the number of rejects, planning a benchmarking strategy, assembling the right team and the proposal to senior management.

The cooperative spirit of our department and our reputation for quality work is the reason, I believe, for our selection

(The answers appear at the end of this chapter.)

Conducting and Participating in Effective Meetings

Take the following multiple-choice quiz before proceeding to the recommendations for leading and attending meetings:

Which of the following activities do you dislike the most?

(a) **Leaving a 15 percent tip for an arrogant waiter who didn't really "wait" on you but kept you waiting instead.**

(b) **Being told the meal you are raving about was actually fried calf's brains**

(c) Attending meetings that waste your time

(d) Hearing the phrase *just a* in front of the word *secretary*

(e) Taking your children to see Santa and finding that he looks like (and probably is) a teenager, who bears no resemblance to jolly old Saint Nick

If you chose (c), take comfort in knowing you are not alone in your dislike of meetings. The Wharton School of Business, the first college business school in the United States, founded in 1881 at the University of Pennsylvania, has found that, excluding preparation time, senior executives spend twenty-three hours each week in meetings and regard only 58 percent of that time as time well spent. World-famous management consultants have harsh words for meetings:

Peter Drucker:	"A manager spending more than 25 percent of time in meetings is a sign of malorganization."
Robert Half:	"America leads the world not in steel or textile but in meetings. The problem is, how do you export meetings?"
Murphy (of Murphy's Law fame):	"The more boring the subject, the longer the meeting will run."

To capitalize on the human resources investments made in meetings, apply the following recommendations whenever you lead a meeting and suggest them to the leaders of meetings you attend (if they are not already employing these tactics):

☐ Whenever possible, allow attendees two day's notice in advance so that they can rearrange priorities and assemble needed thoughts and materials.

☐ Prepare an agenda (and send it out at least two days in advance), preferably listing the amount of time assigned to each item—for example, "Discussion of parking allocations (20 minutes)." List the entries in order of importance and tell how each will be handled (e.g., "discussion").

☐ Set ground rules, especially if the team meets regularly. Post them in the meeting room or print them on the agenda. The group leader or facilitator should refer to these rules at the beginning of the meeting.

☐ Appoint a time monitor. This person has full authority to limit discussions and remind the leader of how much time is left for a particular agenda item. When that time has been used, the monitor encourages going on to the next agenda item.

☐ Appoint a topic monitor. This person is responsible for keeping the discussion on track. The topic monitor both participates in discussions and listens to them in order to keep the meeting focused on the topic at hand.

☐ Appoint a recorder. This person records the ideas generated during the meeting (on a white board or flip chart) and the actual accomplishments of the meeting. Subsequently the recorder sends out the minutes of the meeting to all interested parties (ideally within twenty-four hours). This role requires extensive responsibility; my recommendation is to rotate the role.

☐ Evaluate the meeting so the meeting leader gets feedback on the value participants accorded to the meeting. One way is to pass out a sheet of paper at the end of meetings with one question on it: "If you did not have to attend this meeting, would you have?" When the no's outweigh the yes's, rethink the meeting approach.

☐ Follow up to ensure that others are following up. Meeting leaders need to prepare for the next meeting soon after the first has ended. For example, periodically check with those who have been assigned action items to determine if they will be ready with their assigned tasks the next time the team convenes.

Selecting a Style

An anonymous sage once commented that every time we put words on paper, we allow others to see inside our brains. For example, here is a single sentence—just thirteen words—a candidate wrote on a job application form when asked why she left her previous position.

The company made me a scapegoat, just like my four previous employers did.

You are able to see inside her brain. Do you like what you see? Would you hire her? To write without being cognizant of the impression we may be creating is to doom ourselves.

When you *are* cognizant, you can decide in advance the type of impression you want your readers or listeners to have about you. Just as your wardrobe contains attire suitable for many occasions—work, sporting events, funerals, weddings, church—so does your vocabulary contain enough choices (one million of them actually) to permit you to pick and choose a style suitable to any occasion.

How would you describe the style of writing in each of the following examples?

Due to the vagaries and idiosyncratic differences in the individual handwriting styles of the members of this department, it is incumbent upon me to advise you that henceforth all interoffice correspondence will either be manually printed or electronically sent.

Circle the words that best describe this style.

elegant	professional	bloated	intelligent	light
pompous	confusing	irreverent	feisty	vigorous
gutsy	interesting	long-winded	dense	apologetic

They were polite sometimes but most of the time their demeaning glances brought snowflakes to my heart. I learned to live without them. I became a dentist. But—despite the beautiful villa I have adorned with roses—I could attract the eye of no woman except Maria, who outweighs me by eighty pounds and outstands me by a full six inches. Such is my fate in life, to be engaged in a daily struggle with this woman, locked together in a tiresome, tireless pirouette that ends, with each sun's fiery setting, in the ugliest of ballets. Everything is skirmish and scraps.

Circle the words that best describe this style.

elegant	poignant	bloated	intelligent	light
pompous	confusing	irreverent	poetic	vigorous
gutsy	intriguing	evocative	dense	apologetic

So what's the point? What's the purpose? What's the protoplasm on which the corporate body depends? Well, if you really wanna know, I really wanna tell you. The basic premise here is zero defects. That's right, zero defects. No, you don't need to get your ears checked but you might want to get your checks earmarked for more training in Total Quality.

Circle the words that best describe this style.

tough	light	bloated	informal	conversational
pompous	casual	irreverent	feisty	vigorous
gutsy	interesting	fast-paced	dense	amusing

Think about the various people to whom you typically address your communications. List those in positions higher than your own.

_____

_____

_____

What style would you use with such readers or listeners? _____

_____

_____

Which of your communications, e.g., reports, memos, or letters, are lateral (designed for those whose position within the organization is comparable to your own)? _____

_____

_____

What style is most appropriate for these communications? _____

_____

_____

Audience is but one consideration when you make decisions about style. The others are the medium and the message. Different forms of communications are suited to different styles. For example, a faxed or e-mail communication tends to be more informal than a letter. A communication regarding the company softball game will be more personal than a legal letter of intent.

Give some thought to the match between audience, medium, and message by indicating what medium you would use—e.g., e-mail, memo, letter, bulletin board, one-on-one conversation, staff meeting, company newsletter—and what audience you would seek to address for each of these messages:

Message	Medium	Audience
Notice of retirement party	_____	_____
Change in date of scheduled meeting	_____	_____
Lunchtime lecture on EEO issues	_____	_____

Message	Medium	Audience
Announcement of upcoming training programs	_____	_____
Dates you've chosen for your vacation	_____	_____
Announcement about a used vehicle for sale	_____	_____
Company picnic	_____	_____
Volunteers needed for Adopt -a-School Program	_____	_____
Upcoming audit	_____	_____
Baked goods sale	_____	_____

Addressing Groups, Small and Large

Few other things demonstrate the talent of an empowered assistant more than her ability to stand before a group and share information, inspiration, or entertaining thoughts. Having poise, appropriate gestures, and good eye contact, however, does not mean your audience will be informed, inspired, or entertained. If your presentation is not organized, if you have not done your homework, if your visual aids are not professional or legible, all the poise in the world will not compensate for inadequate preparation.

Five hundred years ago, William Shakespeare warned his compatriots to "mend your speech a little, lest it may mar your fortunes." The Department of Labor deems speech essential to 70 percent of the jobs we Americans perform. Whether the speaking means merely conversing with colleagues or making a formal address to a large group, there are certain guidelines that apply:

- *Consider your audience.* Whether it's a small group at the weekly staff meeting or an assemblage of hundreds, you will have to answer the same set of questions about each audience:

—Who are they?

—Why are they here?

—What are they interested in?

—How much do they already know about the subject?

—How many will be present?

—What will they want to hear?

—What *don't* they want to hear?

- *Organize your remarks.* Having a purpose and being familiar with the subject are necessary but not sufficient conditions for an excellent address. You will have to organize your thoughts. These are some of the most common organizational patterns.

—*General to specific.* This pattern begins with a broad generalization and moves on to substantiate the generalization with specific details.

—*Specific to general.* The buildup that comes with this pattern is especially useful when you want to surprise or even shock your audience into action. The statistics or facts are used as a transition to the main point.

—*Comparison/contrast.* The speaker points out the similarities and the differences between two occasions, people, or products.

—*Demonstration.* Especially in sales presentations, the demonstration is what the audience needs in order to be convinced of the merits you are endorsing.

—*Problem-solution.* For motivational speeches in particular, when you wish to call your audience to action, begin by describing the seriousness of a situation and then move on to specify what can be done about it.

—*Chronological.* Use this to trace the history of a current event or issue.

Whatever approach you use, follow the popular exhortation: "Tell 'em what you're going to tell them. Then tell 'em. Finally, tell 'em what you told them."

- *Grab attention at the beginning. Recapture it at the end.* Your opening and your closing are your first and last opportunities to get your point across. Some of the most popular attention getters are these:

—An anecdote

—Appropriate humor

—A quotation

—A gimmick

—A question

—A statistic

—An interesting graphic

- *Time your presentation before you give it.* The standard vaudeville act was only twelve minutes, for a very good reason: It is hard to keep an audience's interest for much longer than that. (The shortest inaugural address in our nation's history was George Washington's: only 135 words. The longest was William Henry Harrison's in 1841. It was delivered in the dead of winter for two hours. Harrison caught cold the next day and died a month later of pneumonia!)

- *Engage in some warm-up activities—just before you speak.* In order to develop the resonance in your voice, place one hand on your stomach and the other on your chest. Then repeat, "Slow. Slow. Slow." You will feel the resonance in your chest.

—Speak in an exaggerated fashion, so that when you return to your normal tones, you will feel comfortable but more receptive to the use of distinct vocal and physical expressions.

—To improve enunciation, count to 10 silently, enunciating so precisely that others can read your lips. Then say the numbers aloud, using the same lip movements. In front of a group, you would not enunciate quite this much, but the practice will help you eliminate the "lazy-lip" syndrome.

- *Acknowledge that a little tension is quite natural.* In fact, it is preferable to no tension at all. When you are so utterly relaxed that you feel no nervousness whatsoever, you may come across as bored, arrogant, or disrespectful. The late newscaster Edward R. Murrow defined tension as the "sweat of perfection." Your desire to do well is what makes you nervous. Recognize that and remind yourself that nerves are not your enemy. They are the auxiliaries that will make you outstanding.

- *Don't ever read your speech* (unless you are presenting at a technical symposium). People have come to hear you speak. If you intend to merely read, you may as well just pass out the speech and let them read it themselves. Instead, be natural, be yourself. Try to imagine that you are addressing acquaintances socially in a cozy setting. Be as expressive as you usually are. Smile as you normally would. Move your hands the way you always do. Let your voice sound the way it does in less formal circumstances. Talk to your audience about this subject that you know so well. Ideally, it is a subject about which you have strong feelings. Your passion will be heard. Your belief in what you are saying will help convince others that the topic is important.

- *Watch your audience's body language.* If you see them starting to get restless, looking at their watches or at the door, or even nodding off, you will have to change the tone of the address or end a little sooner than you had planned to.

- *Appear to be comfortable, even if you are not.* If your audience senses you are nervous, they will be too.

Projecting Telephone Professionalism

Whether the customer is internal or external, whether the call is for you or your boss, whether the caller is trying to sell something or hoping to buy something—when you conduct business on the phone, your individual transaction is viewed as a reflection of the entire organization. Treat a caller rudely, and the person will assume the entire company is not worth doing business with. Treat a caller well, and you create a favorable impression of your whole organization.

Think about times you have been treated unprofessionally by a telephone representative, of your own company or a different one. How did you feel by the end of the call? What impression did you have of the company as a whole? Then read these six telephonic horror stories that either cost an employee a job or cost the company good customer relations.

A senior vice president in a major southern California aerospace firm called the manufacturing department for information. The person who answered the phone had been hired recently and was not familiar with the names of senior executives. The vice president began the conversation by stating, "This is John Smith."

To which the person at the other end of the line responded, "So?"

A very competent (but not especially grammatical) switchboard operator in a multinational firm received a call from an upper-echelon official in the Canadian corporate office. The caller asked for the general manager of the regional location.

To which the switchboard operator replied, "He ain't done come back from lunch yet."

A caller to an entertainment industry firm asked for Miss Smith, a vice president in charge of production.

The caller was told, "She's in the toilet."

A caller to a real estate firm asked for a person in the Accounts Payable Department.

He was told without preamble, "Oh, she died last week."

A caller to (and potential new customer of) a tax preparation firm asked to speak with the senior auditor.

To which the telephone operator announced, "Oh, he quit last week. He's the third person to quit this month. No one stays here very long."

Individual employees can create powerful impressions of the organization for which they work. That impression can be quite negative if the employee has not been trained to present the company well. If you are curious about how your firm is being represented, make an anonymous call and see how well you are treated.

Are you and your coworkers projecting professionalism? Do callers hang up the phone feeling that they have been well treated? Do employees of your firm attempt to project a "wow factor"—a feeling that the caller is indeed important to the firm?

Analyze your own telephone personality. What specific behaviors of professionalism or nonprofessionalism do you exhibit? Have you ever engaged in any of these "avoid-at-all-cost" actions on the phone? If so, place a checkmark in the box.

Chewing gum while speaking	☐
Inhaling deeply on a cigarette	☐
Interrupting	☐
Being rude	☐
Not being clear when giving information	☐
Not recognizing the name or voice of frequent callers	☐
Not listening carefully	☐
Projecting "tele-phoniness" (sounding *too* poised or *too* well bred)	☐

Eating while carrying on a conversation ☐

Shuffling papers or continuing to work at a keyboard while speaking ☐

Sounding bored ☐

Speaking too quickly or too slowly, too loudly or too softly ☐

Not knowing how to spell common words ☐

Laughing (at a joke heard) as you answer the phone ☐

Putting the caller on hold before he has had a chance to speak ☐

Placing callers on hold for an inordinate period of time ☐

Relying on stock phrases ("Have a nice day.") ☐

Using a speaker phone unnecessarily ☐

Drinking coffee loudly enough to be heard ☐

Addressing the caller as *honey, dear,* or *baby love* ☐

By no means is this an exhaustive list of telephone etiquette transgressions. As you add to it, mentally or physically, promise yourself you'll always epitomize the opposite of what is listed. Having sensitized yourself to the "don't" actions, you should find the "do" list that follows quite to your liking. Check the entries that reflect practices in which you currently engage.

Have paper and pencil at the telephone. ☐

Answer the phone promptly. A phone that rings and rings leaves the caller wondering what is happening on the other end of the line. ☐

Answer properly. Acceptable greetings include: "Good morning. ABC Properties. May I help you?" or "ABC Properties. This is Andrea. How can I help you?" ☐

Use body language to help you convey a receptive, welcoming tone. Actually shrug your shoulders before picking up the phone as a way of separating yourself from the work you are doing. Smile before you begin; many expert telephone salespeople (as well as voiceover artists) use the same gestures they would use if others were actually in the room with them. ☐

Make certain your tone of voice is professional, enthusiastic, and helpful. Do not sound annoyed or uncaring. ☐

Never put the person on hold without first finding out who the person is or what she needs. (The call may be an emergency call, for example, and valuable time could be wasted if the person is on hold.) You may wish to ask if the person would prefer to be called back or to be placed on hold. ☐

Obtain the person's name, and use it during the conversation.

Do not permit a perceptible change in your voice once you learn the person's name. Be courteous to everyone. ☐

Concentrate on the call. Give your fullest attention to the caller, and listen carefully. Do not be distracted by the environment. If necessary, control that environment before continuing the call. If, for example, others are talking loudly beside you, signal to them that you need quiet. Or, if yours is a constantly ringing phone, you may have to forward calls for a half hour or so in order to focus your attention on especially important ones. If your desk faces a doorway, you should probably turn it so that others do not pop in or call to you while you are on the phone. ☐

Use courteous and comforting language, especially if the caller is upset. ☐

Don't make promises or speak on behalf of others. ☐

Avoid slang or jargon the caller may not understand. ☐

Offer to take a message rather than suggest the person call back. (The callback suggestion implies the caller's time is less valuable than your own.) ☐

Write quickly, reducing the message to bare essentials. (You can go back later and fill in the details.) ☐

Consider using an answering machine, if only for a specified period of time during the day. You will be freed to work without interruption. And, believe it or not, some callers prefer to state their message simply and then await a callback if necessary. ☐

Ensuring That Follow-Up Occurs

One hallmark of the truly empowered is the ability to get things done. This ability, alas, is not totally dependent on your own efficiency. Often, your efficiency (or inefficiency) is the result of other people's efficiency (or lack thereof). The observation that "results depend on relationships" packs considerable truth into its four-word declaration.

When relationships are developed in order to get things done, then power is being used in an optimal fashion. Most relationships are based on the advantages each party can bring to the other. We complement each other's needs, and in so doing we develop trust and a healthy dependency on one another. Having built strong interpersonal bases, we can call on other powers that be whenever we need to be fully empowered. Achievement is not a solo act; it is the union of many positive forces. It is teamwork, synergy, and the galvanizing of human resources.

Developing a sense of obligation in others is one way to increase your own power—that is, the ability to effect positive results. When others are obligated to you for help you have extended to them in the past, then you can call on *them* for help *you* need now. This power exchange lies at the heart of the familiar sayings, "You scratch my back and I'll scratch yours" and "One hand washes the other." Doing favors (which often cost very little but are genuinely appreciated) for others essentially means that we expect others to do favors for us at some point in the future.

The purpose of these gestures is the development of friendships with those on whom you depend. Such trade-offs are neither deceptive nor self-aggrandizing. They are a socialized means of survival. In business settings, we develop these relationships because, in part, we need a network of acquaintances on whom we can rely when we need them. And they know they can rely on us.

Secretaries who work for top executives have a great deal of importance in the organization. They frequently have the ear of the chief executive officer and so in some ways wield more clout than do midlevel managers. By virtue of their titles, executive assistants really are in the managerial ranks. Their friendship is worth cultivating on many levels—as models, as mentors, as friends.

Others in the organization are also important to the secretary hoping to make full use of empowerment opportunities. If people in other departments like you, they will often be willing to go a little bit out of their way when you are in a pinch. Calling on them excessively is unkind and unfair, and such one-way selfishness will soon backfire. But if you are there to assist others in their time of need, you can generally expect favors to be returned.

You will need to organize a private follow-up system, using such tools as calendars, to-do lists, and tickler files. The following recommendations will assist as you polish your people skills in order to polish your performance:

- Be direct. Forthright statements, such as "I need your help," generally cause others to want to help you.

- *Don't take advantage of other people's kindness.*

- Sincerely express your appreciation—by a simple thank-you, a card, a small gift, a single flower, a letter, or speaking well of the person to others.

- Check on the progress of work that you need in order to complete your own. A phone call made before the last minute can save both parties considerable turmoil.

- When crises do occur, don't strain relationships by making the situation even more intense. Keep your temper and tongue under control. Becoming insistent or shrill will not make others work any faster. It may, in fact, do just the opposite.

Answers to the Exercise on Page 49

1. Each of us in the accounting offices *looks* forward to meeting you and *welcoming* you to our organization.
   [The subject of the sentence—*each*—is singular, and so the verb—*looks*—must be singular as well. To keep the syntax parallel, both verbs must be written as gerunds: *meeting* and *welcoming*.]

2. To maximize our efforts, *we will reserve the conference room* for the entire day.
   [This error, the dangling infinitive, is one of the most frequent yet one of the most difficult to spot. An easy way to check is to remember

that whoever is doing something *before* the comma should be the same person doing something *after* the comma. In other words, ask who wishes to maximize efforts: the conference room or human beings? Of course, it is the individuals who work in the organization, and so the sentence must be reorganized to bring the infinitive—*to maximize*—closer to the subject.

3. The rationale *is* that an informal atmosphere is most conducive to analyzing the data, which *are* certain to be overwhelming.

    [Every sentence needs a subject and a verb to be complete. *Being* is not a verb; it is a verb form. The second error in this sentence can be found in the word *data,* which is plural for the word *datum.* As such, it needs the plural form of the verb. In more foarmal, technical settings, *data* is used as a plural; in everyday expression, it is used as a single noun.]

4. We *wish* to discuss the following with you: monitoring the number of rejects, planning a benchmarking strategy, assembling the right team and *making* the proposal to senior management.

    [*Anxious* implies anxiety; a better expression would be "We are eager" or "We wish." "We are anxious" is not really wrong, but it does not reflect the excellence to which secretarial exemplars aspire. The second error is one of parallelism again. All the other items on the discussion list are written as gerunds, but *proposal* was listed as a noun.]

5. The cooperative spirit of our department and our reputation for quality work *are* the reason, I believe, for our selection.

    [This is a difficult error to spot. When you have two items listed as the subject—*spirit* and *reputation*—then the verb must be plural— *are*—and not singular, as it originally was.]

If you found all eight, your grammar skills are outstanding. You probably could be doing more of your boss's writing than you currently do. Empower yourself! If you enjoy writing (and you probably do if you have mastered its mechanics), ask to be given more communications tasks.

If you were able to spot only four or fewer (note I did not say *less*), it may be time to take a refresher course in grammar. If your company does not sponsor one, there are numerous training companies that do. There are other possibilities too: get a book from the library, buy an audiotape, or ask the best grammarian you know to be your mentor. By the way, if you don't know why I didn't say *less*, any of these sources can tell you.

Think about it: Every time you put words on paper, you are letting others see inside your brain. Will they see organization, correctness, carefulness, and pride? Or will they see errors, sloppiness, and a lack of professionalism? (Experts have concluded that two or more errors on résumés or cover letters decrease by 80 percent the likelihood that you will obtain the job you are seeking.)

When you write, you are making a statement not only about yourself but about your organization. To illustrate: Would you hire the company that proclaims in its advertisements, "Each of our associates are committed to providing you with error-free work"? In the very sentence that promises no errors, there is an error! Did you spot it? The word *are* should have been *is*. Why? Again, consult one of the sources mentioned earlier.

Tips From Gerri Coleman
Executive Assistant to John Sculley,
Chairman and CEO
Sculley Associates, Inc.

When the term *secretary* is used, I think of someone whose job consists of typing, shorthand, filing, answering phones, photocopying, etc. The titles senior secretary and administrative assistant, however, convey a totally different image. In my position as executive assistant, I certainly use my secretarial skills, but that area of work is minimal compared to the full scope of my job.

How people conduct business today is drastically changed from how they did so in the 1980s. Managers today use computers, and they usually type their own correspondence. They use fax machines, portable phones, pagers, beepers, electronic mail, and, of course, voice messaging systems. All of this, I believe, spells the need for changes in the way secretarial positions are viewed today.

Excellent communications skills are supremely important for secretaries and assistants. Other needed skills include:

- Good common sense

- High degree of confidentiality

- Sensitivity

- Thorough knowledge of grammar

- Ability to serve as a team player

- Understanding of the business

- Good "people" skills

- Organization

- Initiative

- Respect for peers; willingness to help them succeed

- Ability to prioritize

- Proficiency at handling multiple tasks

As you can see from this list, a secretary/assistant today is expected to be a partner to her manager or executive. There is not an executive or junior executive alive today who can succeed without a loyal and devoted assistant. The fact that remuneration levels need to change speaks for itself.

Ours is not the same job it was a few years back. The whole role of a secretary/assistant has become a lot more prestigious and much more respected by senior-level executives because of the close involvement and partnerships that have developed. For those who want to pursue being a secretary/assistant as their life's work, then their work is cut out for them. With this commitment comes a commitment to self: the secretary/assistant will need to show her value to her own manager.

The new role of the assistant is demanding. It requires managerial skills along with the more traditional skills cited earlier. The new role needs to be projected with a new outlook. Only then will this position gain respect from the business community.

4

Maintaining Composure

Handling Information Overload

Do you sometimes feel like a snowflake in an avalanche of information? If so, you should know that the avalanche is getting bigger and more powerful by the moment. Futurist Marvin Cetron, president of Forecasting International, predicts that all the technological knowledge we possess today is equivalent to only one percent of the knowledge that will be available in the year 2050. You thought libraries contained vast amounts of information? Try surfing the Internet! Do you remember a time when television viewing was limited to the three major channels? Projections for the very near future have us surfing through five hundred possible channels.

To extend the snowflake imagery even further, consider the observation that an individual snowflake is one of the most delicate of natural occurrences, yet when snowflakes stick together, their power is absolute and overwhelming.

Sometimes you may feel lost and even isolated in this blizzard of information. The truth is, teamwork can help you find your way out. A team that sticks together can handle the data-drenches much better than one person engaging in a solo struggle. How can you energize your coworkers to reduce the blizzard of data to manageable flurries?

1. *Ask around.* Send out memos or electronic notices. Learn if others are having the same difficulty you are. If so, invite them to join you in efforts to take charge of this chaos.

2. *Point out the WIFM (What's In it For Me?) factor.* By specifying the benefits each and all can derive from such collegiality, you can more easily convince others to join you.

3. *If possible, obtain support from upper management for your efforts.* If your bosses agree to have you meet every Friday afternoon for this empowered undertaking, you will be able to convene much more easily.

Once you have assembled a team, discuss possibilities for empowerment such as the following:

- Jointly subscribe to a publication aimed at your level and to another aimed at one level above (e.g., *The Take Charge Assistant* and *Executary*). On a rotating basis, one person reads the above-level publication, and routes relevant articles both for the members of the group and their managers. Another person, also on a rotating basis, scans the secretarial publication, announces the most relevant titles, and assigns various articles to members, who report on what they have learned the next time the group convenes.

- When workshops or seminars are held, one member attends, takes excellent notes, and then shares what she has learned with other members of the group. The next time a training opportunity arises, a different member of the group attends.

- Each month, a different person learns all she can about relevant subjects from traveling on the Information Highway. At the end of the month, she makes a report and distributes it to the other members of the group.

- On a rotating basis, various members attend meetings of professional organizations and report back to the group what they have learned.

You can also work in concert with your boss in an effort to reduce the overload for yourselves and others.

- Take your manager's name off mailing lists that send unimportant materials and off internal routing lists as well (with her permission, of course). Your company probably has a policy regarding Internet usage. If not, empower yourself to write it, but submit it for approval before disseminating it. Typically, these documents identify the most valuable electronic resources.

- *Smart stealing* is a synonym for the kind of sharing or benchmarking encouraged by quality advocates. Contact other secretaries in other departments or other organizations, learn what they are doing, and then present the best and most workable of those ideas to your boss.

- Ensure that e-mail messages leaving your office are clear in their intent. If they do not contain enough information for the readers to act on them, the result is the generation of *more* e-mail messages to explain what the initial ones did not.

- Avoid electronic overload. You and your boss can suppress the urge to demonstrate unnecessary diligence and refrain from sending irrelevant messages to those who can live without them.

And you can undertake your own campaign to prevent yourself from sinking into the quicksand of data.

- Every six months, determine your most important goals in relation to the work you are expected to do. Then filter all incoming information on the basis of its relevance to those goals.

- Steel yourself against the desire to acquire. As tempting as it may be to obtain all the data you possibly can on a subject, know that you cannot ever know all there is to know. Limit your time, your access, and your totals when it comes to researching.

- Set aside time each day to file. Periodically, go through your files and discard most of the ones you haven't used in a year (use your judgment here). Experts tell us that up to 80 percent of the files we have established are not even used once they have been set up. (Avoid the temptation to do what film producer Samuel Goldwyn asked his secretary to do: "We've got 25 years' worth of files out there," he told her, "just sitting around.

Now what I want you to do is to go out there and throw everything out—but make a copy of everything first!")

• Organize both your tangible and your computerized files. Time management researchers have studied the waste associated with searching for missing files and have learned that it averages to over forty-five minutes a day of the executive's time and his assistant's time. Totaled, this is over a whole month of lost time each year.

• Learn to be a more efficient reader. Take courses or simply practice on your own, and learn to synthesize information more quickly. Relieve stress for yourself and enable your boss to act more quickly by screening, summarizing, highlighting, and then prioritizing the information coming into the office.

Using Nonverbal Language, Paralanguage, and Object Language

Nonverbal Language

We are often unaware of our nonverbal language, but because we use it so frequently and automatically, it is a language with inflections we should be very attentive to. As you read the following suggestions for understanding this special language, place a checkmark in the box if you are already practicing this particular suggestion.

Take in all the body and facial expressions you observe in someone speaking with you. Add them together to obtain a composite impression of the message the other person is sending. Any one may be misinterpreted, but the totality (especially if it is ongoing or frequently repeated) usually signals a clear intent. □

Pay particular attention to eye contact. A person who has trouble looking you directly in the eye may feel uncomfortable in your presence, for any number of reasons. Someone who looks at the ceiling as you are speaking may be signaling that your information is not particularly important. Looking down to the floor is a behavior that people who are literally "feeling down" engage in. Rapid eye blinking often tells us the other person is experiencing some anxiety. If you sense the other person is not especially receptive to your words, you can either ask directly—"John, I get the impression that my words are causing you some difficulty"—and then listen as the other person explains how he feels. Or you can postpone the conversation until a better time. □

Body stance can be quite revealing. A person conversing in a relaxed, informal fashion probably feels very comfortable in your presence. By contrast, if her arms are folded across her chest, her body is partially turned away from you, she is sitting on the edge of her seat, she frequently glances at her watch, she is tapping her foot, or she is otherwise fidgeting, she is not paying very much attention to your words. You may have to involve her more by talking less, or you may wish to consider another way to get your message across, such as presenting it in a written or electronic communication. □

Paralanguage

Para is a Greek prefix meaning "around," "surrounding," or "going beyond." *Paralanguage* means not *what* we communicate but *how* we communicate— the manner of delivery. It encompasses, for example, the use of silence, the speed with which you utter your words, the inflection you bring to them, or the intensity of your speech. It also includes hearing between the lines: If the person who answers your call is speaking while chewing gum or laughing at something someone nearby has said, this paralanguage is telling you that at the least she is not paying attention and at the worst that your call is totally unimportant to her.

As you read the following guidelines for extending professionalism to your paralanguage, place a checkmark in the box next to the items you already know about or are already practicing.

> Conduct a small survey on paralanguage. Make ten phone calls (to people in your own company or in others), and note the qualities that spell professionalism and those that do not. Compare yourself to the best that you hear and consciously strive to incorporate particular elements into your own style.

> Determine how your voice sounds over the phone. Frantic and rushed? Friendly? Polished and professional? Too "bouncy" or too flirtatious? Tape-record yourself. Then ask ten acquaintances to evaluate the tape recording (anonymously, if possible) using this form:

This voice sounds:

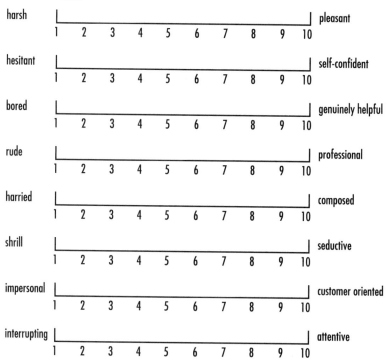

Repeat the exercise in six months with ten different evaluators. This time, though, ask for their input regarding ways to improve. ☐

Conduct an informational interview with someone (inside your own organization or not) whom you regard as possessing remarkably effective paralanguage abilities. You will gain important information on how to improve your own skills in this area. But you will gain even more: Setting up and then doing the interview marks you as an empowered, entrepreneurial secretary, one who is interested in learning. You will increase your network by one—and an important one at that. ☐

Object Language

You cannot *not* communicate. Your object language, i.e., everything about you, says something. If a stranger were to enter your home, the objects there would speak volumes about who you are, what you do, and what you value. These objects, in a sense, have a language of their own: They bespeak your interests, your hobbies, your relationships, etc. Much the same is true for your garage, your car, your work space, and other parts of your life on which you have left your mark.

As you read the following recommendations for using object language to promote your empowered status, check off those you are already doing.

Dress at the level to which you aspire. If you are interested in rising to the level of executive assistant, note the attire of other executive assistants, and pick up clues regarding how to dress. ☐

Consider the way your office looks. Stacks of files on every conceivable flat surface indicate you are a busy person, but they probably also mark you as a disorganized person. Look at what adorns your walls, your desk, your furniture. There is nothing wrong with having stuffed animals in your work area. In all likelihood, however, the offices of those whom you most admire for their professionalism are not filled with cutesy objects. Having certificates from courses you have completed hanging on your walls is a good idea. Not only do they demonstrate your desire for continuous improvement, they also serve as conversation starters and suggest that you have competence in certain areas.   ☐

Ask what others see when they look at you. When you walk, what do you have in your hands? Loose papers rather than a briefcase? Nothing rather than a current business best-seller? A cigarette rather than a gym bag? All the objects that constitute your persona are telling others a great deal about what is important to you.   ☐

Thinking on Your Feet

Whether you are explaining to your boss a project you'd like to pursue; whether you are in a job interview or media interview; whether you are on the phone or on the podium, in the classroom or the conference room—you never know when you will be asked a difficult question or invited to say a few words. Instead of fumbling or mumbling, stumbling or bumbling, there are things you can do to project a confident, competent image.

Consider two examples. The first is of a famous secretary to an infamous televangelist, who was asked if she thought she was intelligent. "Well, I'm not a *bimbo*," she replied. (Somehow, the word *bimbo* suggests bimbo, don't you think?) Contrast that with this young secretary in a Fortune 500 manufacturing firm, who was asked by her boss if she thought she was intelligent. "To me," she replied, "intelligence means knowledge. And I know more today than I knew yesterday."

Before reading the recommendations for developing your quick-wittedness, you should know that studies have found that individuals with transfer support are much more inclined to develop new habits and apply new knowledge than are individuals who do not have such support. The number of support organizations flourishing throughout the world attest to the success of transfer support. Alcoholics Anonymous, Weight Watchers, Parents Without Partners, and many other such groups succeed because their members are willing to assist one another in their attempts to improve their behavior. You don't have to join a formal organization, however. If you can find support among friends, family, and colleagues, you can make the necessary transfers that allow knowledge and desire to become new ways of thinking and acting. Think of the transfer support you can establish. Who is likely to aid you in the skill-building recommendations that follow? How could such individuals support you?

- *When you are thrown by an unexpected question or comment, throw it back on the shoulders of the person who gave it to you in the first place*—for example:

    I'm not quite certain what you mean by morph models.

    On what data are you basing your opinion?

    Is this a personal observation, or do you think it's widely held?

    Could you explain that a bit further?

You'll buy some time to think about your response, and you'll force the other person to clarify his point so that you can answer with the kind of detail he is seeking.

- *Develop your vocabulary.* You'll boost your self-confidence, which always permits you to handle difficult situations more easily, and increase the tools available at your fingertips (or your tongue tip). Every week, vow to learn and use five-to-ten new vocabulary words. Where can you find them? They're as close as your dictionary.

- *Anticipate what might be said, done, or asked and have a few perfect responses ready.* For example, each of us from time to time is asked a question we find rather personal. It is easy to say, "That's none of your business." However, the phrase sounds a bit belligerent and might alienate those with whom you need to maintain good relationships. If you had a stock phrase ready—such as "Do I really have to answer that?" (said with a smile and a playful intonation)—the other person is likely to back off. Another phrase you can use in answer to an intrusive question is, "I'll never tell" (again, sweetly said).

- *Practice speaking.* Write one hundred topics on one hundred different scraps of paper and put them in an envelope. Then when you are on hold or sitting on a bus or otherwise unoccupied, choose one of the topics and devise an impromptu speech based on it.

- *Develop your verbal fluidity.* There are numerous ways to do this, including setting a timer for two minutes and trying to list twenty words that:

    — Have three letters and name an animal (*cow*, for example)

    — Start with *b* and refer to feelings

    — Rhyme with *deal*

    — Have two syllables and relate to work

    — Begin with G and refer to a geographic setting

    — End in *ty* and relate to maturity

    — Have the same two letters or vowels in the middle of the word

    — Start with *a* and pertain to leadership

  Do this exercise at least once a week. (Involving friends, family, or co-workers makes it even more enjoyable.)

  Another way is to write as many sentences as you can in a five-minute time frame using the formula A-B-C-D-E. Each sentence has only five words; the first word begins with the letter A, the second with a B, the third with a C, the fourth with a D, and the last word in each sentence must begin with an E. One possibility is, "All boys carry delicious eclairs." When you tire of the A-B-C-D-E set, try any other; F-G-H-I-J works just as well.

- *Memorize a few anecdotes and use them to extricate yourself from difficult situations.* Let's say a coworker has expressed puzzlement over something you have done. By telling this anecdote, you will bring a bit of levity to the moment for both of you and make your point in a nonabrasive manner:

    A Chinese servant asked his master for permission to attend a friend's funeral. "Yes, of course," agreed the master. "I suppose you will follow that foolish custom of placing food on the grave, too," he added. When the servant said he planned to, the master inquired with a laugh, "And when do you suppose your friend will eat the food?"

    The servant thought for a moment and then replied, "When your wife smells the flowers you brought to her grave last week."

- *Gain practice at thinking on your feet.* Make a collection of the twenty nastiest insults you have heard. Have a friend do the same. (For example, before a staff meeting and in the presence of the director, one woman complimented another on the dress she was wearing and then said, "I wish I could wear cheap clothes as well as you do." Or this: A manager said to a colleague who was just standing to give a report, "I hope your proposal has fewer wrinkles than your shirt.") When the lists are complete, exchange them, and write as many appropriate responses as you can in five minutes.

- *Anticipate your questioners.* The next time you have a presentation to make, do what presidents have long done in preparation for press conferences: Have coworkers grill you with tough questions, questions that are bound to be asked. This practice equips you to handle your own question-and-answer session with aplomb.

- *Control your nerves,* which will control the muscles of your foot so that you don't insert it in your mouth. Breathe deeply and remind yourself of a number of things:

  — As difficult as the situation is, it won't last forever. (Even the darkest hour is only sixty minutes long.)

  — The other people are only human.

  — Such trying moments are actually good for the soul.

  — Next week, this will seem unimportant.

Managing Stress, Time, Energy, and Priorities

Stress

Studies of thousands of subjects reveal that those who respond negatively to life events are more likely to develop a number of illnesses, the most serious of which is heart disease. If your reaction to a stressful occurrence is to become more stressed, you need to learn and use stress busters.

Your employer too should be concerned about the impact of stress on productivity: $150 million in stress-related claims are filed by American businesses each year. If your organization does not have a wellness program in place, you're lucky in a way. You now have an empowerment opportunity staring

Category

Stressor	Job Demands	Equipment	Relationships With Others	Uncertainty	Deadlines	Intensity (1–5)

you in the face. One fairly easy, inexpensive, but extremely effective stress-reduction effort is the Joy Club at Ben and Jerry's Ice Cream organization. Members meet regularly to find ways to make the workplace more joyful.

On the accompanying worksheet, do a stress analysis. Begin by finding a quiet time and place and imagine an ordinary day at work. In your mind's eye, watch a film of your typical schedule unfold. Then fill in the blanks:

> **List all the stressors that occur. Then check off the relevant categories—for example, which stressors are related to job demands, which ones are related to deadlines—and determine the intensity of the stress you feel on a scale of 1 (little stress) to 5 (extreme stress).**
>
> **What common threads run through the highly stressful events?**
> _____
>
> _____
>
> **What is the primary source of stress: people or job expectations?**
> _____
>
> _____
>
> **Is the stress ongoing?** _____
>
> _____
>
> **How do you react when extremely stressed?** _____
>
> _____
>
> **What are you doing to control the stress?** _____
>
> _____
>
> **What else could you be doing?** _____
>
> _____
>
> **Are you gaining more from the job than it is taking from you?**
> _____
>
> _____
>
> **What have you learned from this exercise?** _____
>
> _____

As you read the following recommendations for controlling stress, check off those you are already doing.

Engage in progressive relaxation. Imagine a calm, serene river flowing slowly through your body, starting with the top of your head and moving languidly all the way down to your toes.   ☐

Don't sweat the small stuff. And remember—apart from good health for you and those you love—it's all small stuff.   ☐

Find someone or something that makes you laugh. Turn to that source often.   ☐

Listen to quiet, soothing music whenever you can.   ☐

Learn not to take yourself or your job too seriously. Focus more on the joys, little and great, in your life.   ☐

Engage in physical exercise at least once a day.

If they know you on a first-name basis at fast-food restaurants, if you constantly work through lunch time, if you don't have time for breaks or vacation, it is time to revamp your priorities. Good health should be at the top. Should it degenerate, should you wind up ill, all the efficiency in the world won't matter. You must be able to report to work in order to work.   ☐

Don't get caught in the "awful-izing" trap—that is, making things worse than they are by exaggerating their importance.   ☐

Keep a private "worry" list. When something is bothering you, add it to the list, and refuse to think about it until an appointed time. Then pull out the list and allow yourself to fret for a designated while.   ☐

Examine your self-expectations. Which are realistic? Which are driven only by your need for perfection in all areas? Imagine yourself kicking the too-demanding goals out of your life. ☐

Time

Time is the most precious of all commodities. Optimize its use.

I know you feel you are already working as hard as you can. I know you are being asked to do the work of not just one but one and a half or even two people. But as well as you do, there is always room for improvement. As you read the following recommendations for using time well so that you will have time for empowerment opportunities, check off those you are already doing.

Find out how you are spending your time. Keep a log for two weeks. ☐

Learn to say no. ☐

Do chunks of the same tasks. For example, if you need to file ten papers in the course of a day, do all ten at once instead of making ten separate trips to the file cabinets. ☐

Keep a to-do list. Update it at the beginning or the end of every day. ☐

Do the most unpleasant task on your list first. (As Mark Twain advised, "If you have to eat a frog, don't stare at it too long.") ☐

Determine which are the "trivial many" aspects of your job. Try to eliminate or streamline some so you can spend more time on the "vital few." ☐

Establish a buddy system. Find a friend who can help you out on those rare occasions when you feel you are going under. ☐

Divide a big project into several short segments and tackle those one at a time. ☐

For one month, get up twenty minutes earlier than usual. Use the extra time wisely. ☐

Ascertain your chronobiological prime time. In other words, at what time of the day or night is your body functioning at peak performance? Do your most challenging work then. ☐

Determine which habits are enslaving you, and break those bonds. If you feel "compelled" into repetitive behavior, if you don't feel "right" skipping a routine (even a pleasurable one), then you are enslaved to some extent. Such compulsive behaviors eat up much of your time and must be recognized when seeking better time management. Try finding equally beneficial alternatives. For example, if you "have" to spend the first half hour of every day drinking coffee and reading the paper, take the coffee on the road with you and catch up on the news by listening to the car radio. Watch less television; do something constructive instead. ☐

Energy

Studies of outstanding leaders reveal that among their diverse and individually admirable traits, one in particular shows up repeatedly: Those who are energetic are not only able to arouse their own passion on behalf of a certain cause, but they manage to arouse the passions of others. Think about a project or hobby that so consumes you that you lose all sense of time when you are doing it. There are many ways to describe this optimal flow, but essentially you find all your physical and mental energies being poured into the pursuit of the moment.

The energy to which I refer is not necessarily equated with being in top physical condition. Franklin D. Roosevelt, after all, was confined to a wheelchair for much of his presidency, and John F. Kennedy suffered from constant back pain. The energy that drives empowered actions is born of commitment and nurtured by conviction.

As you read the following recommendations for maximizing your energy allotment, check off those you are already doing. And remember that energy is not depleted by use. The more you use, the more you get in return.

Regard yourself as a "staminac"; take pride in your ability to be busy without becoming neurotic. ☐

Spread your energy evenly throughout the day rather than release it in spurts. ☐

Figure out what specifically intrigues you about those activities you engage in passionately. If possible, apply the intriguing elements to less interesting aspects of your work. For example, if you enjoy writing the monthly report for your boss, it may not be the actual writing that you enjoy as much as the trust he shows in you by allowing you to work independently. If this is the case, seek other means of operating on an independent, empowered level.

Find a way to give back to others. Those who do volunteer work inevitably find they receive more than they give. Knowing we are needed, learning that we are depended upon and appreciated (if only for one hour a week), keeps our energy flames stoked.

Spend less time sitting. Instead, do something physical—sit-ups or cleaning out drawers or walking in place. If you typically make notes at your desk, try doing some writing by standing and using a cabinet as a writing surface. (Novelist Thomas Wolfe composed his finest works in this manner.)

Figure out how to get more physical activity at work. You may not be able to do push-ups in your office, but you can take the stairs instead of the elevator, or walk at lunch, rather than sit at a desk.

You are what you eat. If you eat heavy meals, you will feel (and possibly look) heavy. Your energy level drops after lunch because of the postprandial letdown. Your body's energies are directed to the digestion of food, thus leaving you feeling tired. The more you eat, the more there is to digest, and the less energy you will have.

Tension is an energy robber. Humor is an energy retriever. Words, actions, and visual images directed at the jocular vein restore your emotional equilibrium and help you move from fatigue to fun, from hostility to humor, from languor to levity. Here's just one example from a job applicant's resumé: *"Reason for leaving: Was met with a string of broken promises and lies, as well as cockroaches."* Collect others and pull them out whenever you need a quick energizer. Better yet, share your collection with others, and ask them for theirs in return.

When your reserves are low, call a friend to boost your flagging spirits. Think back to those times when you simply did not have energy to do something. Then a friend showed up and said, "Oh, let's do it." And you did. From some deep in-

ternal well, companionship evoked strength you didn't think
you had at the time. ☐

Take a five-minute vacation at least twice a day. Give yourself
a mental pep talk, watch goldfish swimming in a bowl, walk
briskly down a long corridor, read several poems, practice your
calligraphy—or do whatever else will help you refocus your
attention and rechannel your energy. ☐

Develop good sleep habits to benefit from sleep's restorative
powers. If poor sleep habits (irregular bedtime, sleeping late
on weekend mornings, staying up late at night, frequent naps
during the day) are leading to poor sleep, then you are not
only sapping your energy but impairing your judgment, thinking, memory, and attention. As a result, you are probably more
irritable and less productive. ☐

Priorities

John Bryan, chairman of Consolidated Food, discusses in one of his brochures
the importance of prioritizing for department managers: "Some people go
through the day just doing their jobs, never realizing there are only two or
three things that are important to this department, and they should do those
first, and [in] the very best [way] they can. Getting them to realize that—
that's running a department."

What would you say are the two or three things most important to your department—whether you are running it or assisting the person who does? Once
you have identified these, ask the same question of your boss, and then compare your list to hers. Propose ways you can take a more active, empowered
role in areas crucial to accomplishing the organization's or department's mission.

Having charted a course, use this schedule for dividing each day:

- Three hours spent on work due today and unanticipated requests
  that need attention today

- Three hours spent on assignments due next week

- One hour spent on deadlines that will fall within the next month

- One half-hour spent on assignments due in six months

- Leftover minutes spent on tasks that will fall due within the next
  year

As you read the following recommendations for determining priorities, check off those you are already doing.

Use questions such as these to determine which of your tasks are priority items:

—What problems can be anticipated? What is the potential here for trouble?

—What needs to be cleaned up or cleared up from the previous day or job?

—Which tasks have opportunities embedded in them?

—Which tasks relate to the mission?

—Which tasks would my boss view as the most vital?

—Which tasks will produce results (rather than simple busyness)?

—Which tasks call for my special talents? □

Take three minutes at the end of each day to review what happened.

—What did I do today?

—Which were the right things at the right time?

—Which were the right things at the wrong time?

—Which were the wrong things at the right time?

—Which were the wrong things at the wrong time? □

Determine criteria for prioritizing. Seek input from your boss, customers, and colleagues. Consider other criteria too (cost, time, value, etc.). □

Decide which of your priorities are the most important. □

Confirm your designations of your top priorities with appropriate others. Seek agreement and alignment before getting too far along. Check with significant workplace others often to see if *their* priorities have shifted. □

Set milestones and get approvals along the way. □

In addition to blocking out priorities on the calendar, block out each day. How much time will you spend on what? Build in extra time for things that can (and usually do) go wrong. ☐

Divide and conquer. Break the work into large chunks, and each chunk into smaller chunks. ☐

Reward yourself (and others who have contributed) as each milestone is met. ☐

Develop a checklist so necessary steps (including approvals) will not be overlooked. ☐

Handling Conflicts With Confidence

"The American people are so tense," Norman Vincent Peale once noted, "that it is impossible to put them to sleep—even with a sermon." The cost of this tension is $17 billion a year in stress-related mistakes, bad decisions, lost time, lower productivity, sickness, and lawsuits. Mission and quality and cost and teamwork and empowerment: all of these are important organization thrusts, but it's hard to explore them when we are fighting one another or stressed to the hilt. After all, how many people can keep up a brave front while being stabbed in the back? How many of us are willing to put oars into troubled waters when the wind is being taken out of our sails? How can we fight fire with fire if we're being burned or, worse yet, if we are burned out?

Sometimes, of course, the source of the stress is beyond your control. In these employment-uncertain times, emotions are close to the surface, and tensions run rampant. Definitions to reflect the possibility of imminent layoffs emerge everywhere: "Will the last person leaving Seattle please turn out the lights?" Or, "Optimists are those who bring their lunch to work. Pessimists are those who leave the car running." Humor helps. So does the reminder that you *always* have choices.

Keep in mind the words of this anonymous sage: "The infinite capacity of human beings to misunderstand one another makes our jobs and our lives far more difficult than they have to be." You can choose to understand.

As you review the following suggestions for handling conflict, place a checkmark in the box if the idea is one you are currently using.

Put the conflict you are having into perspective. Turn on the evening news any night of the week, and see the results of large-scale conflict in places like Bosnia or the West Bank. Know that by comparison, your battle can surely be resolved peacefully. ☐

If you are having a problem with another person, realize that you are 50 percent of the problem—if only in the eyes of the other person. If you are not willing to continue the enmity, then the problem is at least 50 percent resolved. ☐

Ask the other person, "What would you like me to do about this?" If you cannot put sincerity into your voice, wait until you can. ☐

Ask the other person, "What would *you* be willing to do about this?" If you get a less than sincere answer, try again in a week or so. ☐

Think about the big picture. If you have not been able to resolve a conflict with someone at work, the two of you are probably not working as cooperatively as you could. ☐

Less cooperation usually means less efficiency; less efficiency translates to higher costs; lower profits could mean layoffs. If everyone were acting the way you two are, the company would go out of business in a week! For your own good health (if not the company's), it may be wise to swallow your pride instead of leaving it stuck in your craw, where you might choke on it. ☐

Assess your conflict resolution skills. Make a list of the last five conflicts in which you were engaged. How many of those were resolved successfully, with a "win" for both parties? If you were pleased with the outcome of four or five, you possess extensive skills already. Analyze what they are, and work to sharpen them. ☐

If you were not satisfied with the results in the majority of these cases, evaluate what behaviors you may be exhibiting that are blocking resolution. Do you use sarcasm? Are you unwilling to compromise? Do you refuse to listen? Do you have a bad attitude? Self-assessments are never easy, but they are the only place to start if you are serious about making improvements.

Identify your beyond-work skills, and determine which you can apply to conflicts at work. If you coach Little Leaguers, for example, you have learned some things about interpersonal and intrapersonal conflicts. Apply the knowledge gained in some situations to totally different situations.

Have a plan, and propose it to the person with whom you are experiencing conflict—for example, "Let's each focus on one thing we think prevents us from working together more respectfully."

Don't imagine slights that were not intended as such. And if others fail to recognize you or your talents, do not develop ulcers over the lack of recognition. If you allow every honest exchange to become an affront, your health will suffer in no time. Consider if you would have been as offended as John Barrymore apparently was if this incident had happened to you:

> Barrymore was shopping at an elegant clothiers and found a number of articles he wished to purchase. The clerk asked the famed actor his name. The actor's eyebrows rose (as did his blood pressure, no doubt) and, in the haughtiest of tones, he announced the name "Barrymore." The clerk needed more information, however. "Which Barrymore, please?" he politely inquired.
>
> This was more than the world-acclaimed thespian could bear. "Ethel," he intoned before turning on his heel and exiting.

Teddy Roosevelt observed that the person who starts a fight admits he's lost the argument. When your viewpoint differs from another person's—even radically—remember that she is as entitled to that viewpoint as you are to yours. Maintaining such an awareness will prevent discussions from escalating into disagreements, and arguments from escalating into fights.

Have a few choice lines ready—"Can we agree to disagree?"—and use them as the occasion warrants. ☐

Remain centered by recalling the core values with which you were raised: respect, honor, cooperation, concern, dignity. Do not let the behavior of others submerge your basic decency. ☐

Don't respond in kind unless it's kind. ☐

Develop the art of nonprovocative questioning. Questions usually force others to think rationally rather than emotionally, especially if the questions reflect a sincere desire on your part to learn what the other person has to say. ☐

Ann Landers has established Reconciliation Day (April 2) "to heal old wounds and reach out to those with whom we may have lost touch." You need not wait until then to mend and amend fractured relationships. ☐

The broken-record technique works when someone is hurling epithets at you. Keep saying, "Excuse me?" As the disputant repeats the insults and hears how vulgar they sound, he may very well terminate the invectives. ☐

Suggest a truce for a specific period of time. If all goes well, ask that it be made permanent. ☐

Learn to paraphrase the critical elements of the other person's thoughts before countering them with your own. ☐

Use both the Worm's Eye and the Bird's Eye perspectives to put conflict in its rightful place. Answer these questions about a given conflict individually, with your team, and/or with the person who is the source of the conflict. They will help you get a grip on the reality of conflict and the effects it may be having on you and others in the workplace. ☐

Worm's Eye:

• What is the source of this conflict?

• How often does it occur?

• How did it begin?

- Are others having this same problem?

- Do I possess the skills needed to resolve this problem?

- If not, how can I obtain them? Or, who can assist in this situation?

- What would I have to give in order to resolve this conflict?

- What could I hope to gain by resolving this conflict?

- How much of the problem is my problem?

- Would I be embarrassed to have my children (spouse, pastor, parents) know I am engaged in this dispute?

Bird's Eye:

- What are the negative effects of this conflict?

- How does our inability to resolve this make us appear in the eyes of others?

- In the long range of my life, how important is this conflict?

- What is the cost (on health, reputation, office morale, productivity, mission) of letting this conflict continue?

- Is it worth this cost?

- What could be achieved if emotion and energy were not being diverted in this way?

- If a crisis occurred at this moment, could I put the conflict aside to assist the person with whom I am having the conflict?

- What prevents me from assisting without the crisis?

- Five years from now, how important will this conflict be?

Tips From Annette Worth
Executive Secretary to the Partners of
National Training Systems

- I try not to take someone's anger or negativity too personally. Angry people have had plenty of practice on a lot of people before me, and whatever way they react is their modus operandi. Depersonalizing their anger, if only in my own mind, helps me maintain my composure. What helps most is answering in a calm voice and not attacking in retaliation if I have been verbally attacked.

- A lot of stress is self-induced. Much can be avoided by remembering the Golden Rule.

- Maintaining a reputation for fairness and keeping other people's best interests at heart are preventive measures. Although not a guarantee against problems, such efforts often smooth the way when stressful situations arise.

- In order to forgive myself and to avoid having stress from mistakes interfere with my work, I replace negative thoughts with an affirmation that turns my thinking in the right direction.

- "Go jump in the lake," "Go fly a kite," and "Take a hike" are all good suggestions for maintaining composure, in that they are all physical activities. However, they are not too practical for the working hours. A revised version that does help is to take a walk—outdoors is best, but even a walk down the hall is better than letting stress overtake you.

- Stress will take its toll on your physical condition. After a difficult interlude, an energy booster such as fruit will usually restore your equanimity.

- When dealing with complaints, I try to acknowledge the problem by identifying how the person feels, then following up with action. It's important to understand exactly what the problem is without dwelling on it. I get to work fixing the problem and taking steps to ensure the same problem doesn't occur again. Respect and acceptance are what people seek. We can show others we value them by listening. "Listening," as more than one person has observed, "is a form of acceptance."

- Taking a break can be the wrong thing to do if there is a fast-approaching deadline. The half-hour subtracted cannot be replaced. Working through the problem, with a quick diversion now and a longer reward later, is a productive move.

Our staff members came up with additional ideas, such as these:

"I remind myself that if I lose control, I will lose power."

"I choose not to let the details take over. Lists are my salvation. I prioritize and work through one thing at a time when the job seems overwhelming. I look at the big picture. I know I can handle just about anything if there's an end in sight."

"I use humor."

"Years of martial arts and meditation help me remember it's not worth getting upset."

"I tell myself I'm winning. I'm in control. And if I am losing, it's only a battle; it's not the war."

"I take a deep breath and think, This, too, shall pass."

"I focus in on my goals. I center myself in terms of what I want and what my objectives are. I try to stay clearheaded and keep emotions under control so I can think precisely about what I need to do."

"I think about what I am for, not what I am against. The more I think about what I'm for, the more quickly it comes to fruition."

"I realize from experience that a crisis or series of interconnected bad news events may appear more serious at the onset than after I've had a chance to focus. Buy as much time as you can, and solve the problem with the greatest possible benefits flowing to all parties. I stall for time and remain positive."

Tips From Mary Joe Holloway
Executive Secretary to the Partners of
National Training Systems

- I try not to get sidetracked. I pause and tell myself that the situation is only temporary and will be resolved. No matter how difficult the particular problem is, there is always a solution.

- When the air is tense and emotions are evident, I decide not to speak unless it's necessary. And when I do speak, I select my words carefully.

- If a situation arises that needs to be rectified, I ignore whose fault it was and why it happened. Instead, I concentrate on the solution.

- Watching for nonverbal signs is important. So is not displaying any facial expressions myself, for they might be misconstrued, especially when tensions are high.

- When involved in an altercation, I think of the worst-case scenario and realize how much hurt could be caused. This focus helps me to remain calm.

- To help me reach the truth surrounding the problem, I count to ten. Before I say anything, I try to depersonalize the situation and remind myself of the ultimate goal.

- I try to step away from the situation for a moment and mentally regroup.

- During a possible crisis, I consider if there is anyone better qualified than I to handle it. If not, I proceed in the best way I can.

- If I am under attack, I ask to be excused and walk around the building until I regain control.

- On the vanity level, I consciously think about getting physically sick or looking older if I allow myself to be continuously unnerved and upset.

5

Grounding Yourself Against Future Shock

Developing the Requisite Skills

The revolutionary forces at work today will have tremendous impact on how we all do our work tomorrow. Will you be ready? Will you be able to take advantage of the forces such as global competition, technology, and self-supervision? Do the prospects of telecommuting or working as a "freelance bundle of talents" daunt you? Do you know what employers regard as critical, and do your skills match those identified needs?

Where do you begin? Where you have always begun to acquire new knowledge: in books, magazines, and newspapers. Keep your eyes and ears open to emerging trends. In fact, you might form your own internal clipping service. With a group of equally interested secretaries, begin to keep files on articles each of you comes across dealing with skills that will be needed in the future. While there may be some differences of opinion among the experts, there will also be a great deal of similarity. To illustrate, author-consultants Andrew

Sherwood and Roger Flax have identified the most important knowledge areas they see for handling the work of the future. In the blank space to the right of each entry, record the grade you would give yourself in terms of your abilities in the area (note that "Writing" appears on both lists):

Sherwood List		Flax List	
Speaking	_____	Problem solving	_____
Writing	_____	Writing	_____
Interviewing	_____	Time management	_____
Interpersonal	_____		
Training	_____		
Finance	_____		

Next, you may wish to check with your boss, other managers, and those in the human resources department to learn the skills they are stressing now and will be stressing in the future. An extensive study conducted by the American Society for Training and Development found that American employees will need to have a wide range of skills for the future—skills previously held by supervisors alone. (Remember the description of the "managerial milkshake" from Chapter 1?) The seven broad areas encompassing these skills follow. In each blank space, record the grade you would give yourself in terms of your abilities in this area. Then think about the relationship between each of these skills and having an empowered status.

Knowing how to learn _____

Competence: reading, writing, computation _____

Communication: listening, oral _____

Adaptability: creative thinking, problem solving _____

Personal management: self-esteem, goal setting, motivation, employability, career development _____

Group effectiveness: interpersonal skills, negotiation, teamwork _____

Influence: organizational effectiveness, leadership _____

By becoming sensitized to the need to learn more about future skills, you will find more than enough information for determining the direction you need to take. The list that follows was gleaned from various reports. Place a checkmark in the box to the right if you feel you are proficient in the area.

Interpersonal skills ☐

Ability to solve problems ☐

Communication skills ☐

Technical knowledge ☐

Energy level ☐

Judgment ☐

Oral communications ☐

Stress management skills ☐

Understanding of expectations ☐

Ability to make tough decisions ☐

Ability to learn new material in a reasonable time ☐

Ability to work on teams ☐

Perhaps it can all be reduced to Theodore Roosevelt's assertion: "The most important single ingredient in the formula of success is knowing how to get along with people." Even if you lack skill in other key areas, when you know how to relate well with others and how to show appreciation of them, you are able to develop proficiency with their help. Without this skill, you may not be able to learn because others may not be willing to share with you.

The predictions of shortages of skilled laborers are already being realized. There will always be a supply of menial labor, but for jobs that command high salaries, skilled workers will be in demand. Increasingly, jobs call for basic skills and beyond-the-basic skills as well. Witness the clerk who sent a check for $2,200 instead of $22 because she didn't understand decimals. Another such case is the steel worker who was unable to read written instructions and consequently ordered $1 million worth of the wrong product. Billions are lost each year by American business because of such mistakes.

Take stock now of what you have and what you will need. Check with knowledgeable others, read as much as you can, and form an action team (you will no doubt find individuals in your immediate or community environment with a similar interest in expanding their personal portfolios) to do something about becoming prepared for the future, in order to avoid being shocked by it.

Gaining Visibility and Influence

Some people feel that only braggarts make others aware of who they are and what they can do. Certainly there are limits to advertising your talents, but if you are keeping your light hidden beneath the proverbial bushel, then you are keeping everyone in the dark. A good example of speaking up instead of "heaping up" (keeping everything inside—the good ideas and the not-so-good feelings—because you are afraid to express them) comes from the secretary to Supreme Court Justice Ruth Bader Ginsburg. Ginsburg stopped talking about sex discrimination years ago because of something her secretary said: "I'm typing all these briefs and articles for you and the word *sex, sex, sex* appears on every page. Don't you know those nine men [on the Supreme Court] hear that word and their first association is not the one you want them to be thinking? Why don't you use the word *gender*? It will ward off distracting associations."

If you do not have the kind of relationship with your boss that permits open exchanges, you may need to develop your interpersonal skills (note how often they were mentioned in the preceding section) in order to feel free to offer improvement-suggestions to your boss. These tips should help.

- *Deliberately choose the time and place for sharing ideas.* Some secretaries speak without thinking about the boss's circumstances and then wonder why their ideas are not more warmly received.

- *Whenever possible, back up your proposal with statistics* to validate its worth. You may find information about cost savings or time savings, you may find precedents affirming the improvements in productivity, or you may quote others who endorse the kind of thing you are proposing.

- *Explain how your proposal will benefit the boss and the organization.*

- *Take an optimistic approach to your proposal.* Don't ask your boss *if* he would like to hear your idea but *when.* (This is the trick teenagers use when they need to borrow the family car. If they ask, "Can I have the car tonight?" the answer can only be yes or no. But if they assume they can have the car, then they give their parents a choice of the time for returning it, as in, "Dad, I need the car tonight. Can I keep it until 10 or do you need it back before then?") For example, instead of saying to your boss, "I have a good idea about gross purchases. Would you like to hear about it?" say, "I've done some research into gross purchases. I can either share it with you in a report or just run it by you when you have a moment. Which is easier for you?"

If you do have an open relationship with your boss, continue to hone your ideas, and present the best of them to her. There's a caveat to be considered, though, before you decide to bring that light of yours out from under the bushel. Demonstrations of excellence tend to beget requests for other demonstrations of excellence. By making your proficiency visible, you may be creating a monstrous need for that proficiency. At first you will find it flattering, but in time the need for your talents may take time away from the job you are expected to do and thus may cause considerable stress for you, or make you feel you are being used.

If you have learned to say no, if you do not suffer from a "must-please-everyone" mind-set, if you consider your own needs as important as the needs of others, if you can balance your own work needs and the work needs of others, if you can ask for some compensation when it is clear you deserve it, then go ahead and let your talents be known. If you can't do these things, you may be subject to the Yuk effect. (It is derived from an ecologist's attempt to eliminate sugar cane beetles in Australia by placing a new species of toad, affectionately called the Yuk, in the sugar cane environment. Not only did the Yuks fail to destroy the beetles, they multiplied in stunning numbers. Cane sugar farmers then had two problems to deal with: the beetles *and* the Yuks.)

The problem of not being recognized for your talents may lead to being *too* recognized—being overwhelmed by Yuk requests. The solution to a problem may become an even bigger problem than the original problem presented. Understanding the true meaning of empowerment is the key here. If you are empowered to accept new challenges, you are also empowered to *not* accept them.

Here are eight arenas in which you can gain visibility, followed by four case studies for you to think about:

1. *Leadership.* Look around you and listen. Whenever and wherever you learn that things aren't the way they should be, you have an opportunity for leadership staring you in the face or whispering in your ear. (Sam Walton of Wal-Mart fame called it "eliminating the dumb.") Depending on the time you can devote to such high-visibility undertakings, you can select a project such as an annual event, complete and replete with media coverage. Or you can select a smaller project, such as office beautification, with everyone bringing in a plant or helping to take out the trash.

2. *Writing.* Look at publications. With the proliferation of periodicals, the opportunities are ripe, rife, and right for secretaries to express their thoughts and gain visibility (and sometimes extra money) in the process. There are numerous publications (such as the American Management Association's *Take Charge Assistant*) that welcome input from secretaries, to be shared with other secretaries.

3. *Speaking.* Look for upcoming events. America is a nation of conference planners and conference participants. Conferences are being planned within your own organization and industry year-round. If there is no formal event scheduled for Secretary's Week in April, empower yourself to organize a symposium. Demonstrate your leadership by inviting secretaries from other organizations to join you on a panel to discuss

the future of the secretarial profession. This can be a relatively inexpensive undertaking that is bound to bring greater visibility to you and the other secretaries within the organization.

Of course, you may wish to consider going national with your talents. If you enjoy being in front of an audience, you may wish to make a presentation at a state or national conference. Contact the organization sponsoring the event and ask for the request for proposal (RFP) outlining the requirements for speakers at future conferences. In addition to the extensive publicity accompanying such activities, you may even earn some pennies for your thoughts.

4. *Expertise.* Look inside yourself. What is your greatest area of expertise? Can you develop it (or have you already developed it) to the point of being a floating expert? Assuming you want this kind of visibility, keep a journal to record your thoughts regarding the alignment of your expertise with your organization's needs. When you have found a good fit, volunteer to assist—your boss, another secretary, another team. Offer suggestions or actual time; make your presence and your proficiency known.

5. *Teaming.* Look at what teams are being formed. Are any of them taking on improvement projects that interest you? If so, contact the team leader or the person assembling the team, and learn more about the mission. Assuming you can make the kind of time commitment necessary, take an active role in helping to meet that mission. Another possibility is to form a team of your own to explore worthy possibilities.

6. *Professional associations.* Look at what's out there. Consider local, national, and even international organizations that provide members a wide range of benefits centered on a common interest. If your schedule permits, consider not only joining and attending meetings, but volunteering to serve on committees and perhaps even running for office. Visibility through external organizations is an ideal way to gain visibility in your own workplace.

7. *Training.* Look at what vacuums exist. Do an informal needs assessment to learn what kinds of training your coworkers are interested in. Then work in concert with the training department (formally) or on your own (informally) to arrange for lectures, seminars, workshops, demonstrations, and presentations to be delivered to those interested in a given topic.

An example of an informal group you could assemble is a book club. Let us assume you and several other secretaries have noted certain role reversals occurring. Bosses are doing more computerized tasks (sometimes being taught how by secretaries, who are usually the first in departments to receive new systems training), and secretaries are more involved with purchasing or proposals or meetings. Observing the latter's interest in learning more about managerial functions, you could assume an empowered position and arrange for monthly meetings at which management books are discussed, each member sharing information on a different book.

Case Study 1

Cynthia has always prided herself on her creative abilities. When she is asked to join a team to plan events for National Quality Month (October), she accepts readily, believing this to be an opportunity to win friends, influence people, and gain visibility for her talents in the process. At the first meeting, the team leader gives out assignments for action items to be completed. Cynthia is given the unimaginative task of analyzing the results of an employee survey. What should Cynthia do in this scenario?

    (a) Accept the assignment, showing a willingness to be a good team player.

    (b) Ask for a different assignment.

    (c) Ask if the job could be done jointly with another team member—one who is familiar with data analysis.

Case Study 2

Nancy takes pride in her ability to handle virtually any customer complaint. Recently she placated an angry customer so ably that the customer asked to speak with her supervisor. Unfortunately, her supervisor is on vacation for the entire week. What should Nancy do in this case?

    (a) Advise the customer that she appreciates the thought but her supervisor is on vacation.

    (b) Ask the customer if he would be willing to write a letter instead.

(c) Explain that her immediate supervisor is away, but she could transfer the customer to her supervisor's supervisor.

Case Study 3

Juana is conducting an inventory in the stockroom when she inadvertently overhears the chairman's executive assistant telling a vendor that she will be taking an early retirement (and asking him not to reveal her secret). For a long time, Juana has dreamed of having this position. In fact, the extra assignments she has taken on for the past several years were chosen with this goal in mind. She knows she is highly regarded by the chairman and his assistant, but she doesn't know if *they* know how interested she is in the position. What should Juana do?

(a) Meet with the assistant and explain that she overheard her speaking of her retirement plans. Explain her goals to the executive assistant and ask to be considered among the candidates being interviewed for the position.

(b) Work even harder, and hope she will be recognized even more than she already is.

(c) Wait until the opening is announced, and then put in her application.

Case Study 4

Lisa gets along well with everyone in the office but is not overly social because she takes her work very seriously. She would rather give up a chat than be five minutes late with a deadline. Recently her boss asked her to "keep her eyes and ears open" and report back to him about the behavior of one particular manager. Her boss has already met with the manager, sent him to training, and has made the manager (as well as the whole department) aware of the need for professional, respectful treatment of one another. The manager, however, denies he has sexually harassed anyone.

Still, the rumors persist. Fearing the possibility of a sexual harassment lawsuit, the boss wants to have someone watching the behavior of the manager to confirm whether the rumors about him have any foundation. Lisa has never before been taken into the boss's confidence in this way. She wants to assist, but she also wants to be fair; the boss's request seems like spying to her. What should she do?

(a) Refuse to engage in the behavior being asked of her.

(b) Go along with the boss's request, knowing that if the manager is innocent, no harm will come to him and if he is guilty, he deserves to be reprimanded.

(c) Suggest that the boss wait to see if charges will be filed.

(Case study analyses appear on later pages.)

Networking

It's called net*working* for a reason (it's not net-*eating* or net-*sitting* or net-*drinking*). When you are in circumstances that invite you to make professional connections, you cannot simply schmooze with one person the whole time. Networking means work, hard work, to build a net with rope strong enough to catch any potential fall that life is planning for you. No matter how secure your current circumstances appear to be, keep in mind this bit of cosmic insight:

> *Question.* Do you know how to make God laugh?
>
> *Answer.* Tell him your plans.

For businesspeople, the person with the fattest Rolodex wins. What's the prize? you ask. The more people you know, the more easily you can get done what you want to get done. Your goals may center on yourself or others, but the more connected you are, the more support you can garner in relatively short time.

The following suggestions will help you gain visibility. They will enable you to use networks to increase net worth (on levels far beyond the financial).

• *Keep a notebook (or computer database) in which you record all the new contacts you are making.* Jot down names and the places where you met these people, and include interests they may have, the work they do, the exchange that occurred between you. *Exchange* is the operative word here. The network works if both parties are willing to assist one another. A one-directional connection will soon disconnect. There is nothing wrong with determining what your needs are and who can best aid you in fulfilling them. However, your speculation should not stop there. As you plan to be in the right place at the right time, realize that your potential partner is usually there for a reason as well. Ask what you can offer your network partner in turn.

- *Set yourself a goal.* It may be to make a certain number of acquaintances each week or month or at each function. Take an active approach to expanding your connections.

- *Collect business cards.* When you exchange business cards, write on the reverse side of the card the special information you will need to continue the connection in the future (e.g., where and when you met, something the person said, a special interest he revealed, why you would like to keep in touch with him, what you promised to send him).

- *Give yourself enough time to network* by arriving at events early enough to circulate.

- *Don't try to cram business into pleasure time.* Yes, you should exchange cards, but use future appointments to make proposals or pitches.

- *Compile all your past network entries into one centralized file.* As you review the complete file, consider which individuals or types of individuals have assisted you most in the past. Make a concerted effort to meet more of such people in your future networking overtures. Consider, too, which parts of your network need to be revamped or reinforced.

- *Keep in touch with your network acquaintances.* To contact them only when you need assistance smacks of opportunism. Send cards, letters, notes, or e-mail messages regularly. Send out a newsletter, or get together informally. Your overtures are bound to be appreciated.

- *Thank others for the referrals they send your way.* By expressing your appreciation, you'll be in the contact's mind, thus increasing the chances that your name will come to mind when the circumstances are ones you'd be interested in.

- *Be outgoing if you hope to be outstanding.* Wallflowers and empowered entrepreneurs are never one and the same. If you are serious about networking, you must make serious efforts to get to know strangers.

Welcoming Change

It's almost axiomatic to note that the only constant in the world today is change. And yet there are those who foolishly remain fixed in time, hoping to stop the dizzying speed of change. The only way to live nonneurotically in a changing world is to acknowledge—nay, welcome—the change that will be part of our lives for the rest of our lives. As the pundits tell us, "When you're through changing, you're through!"

Acknowledge that the nature of work, the workplace, and the workforce itself is changing. According to projections from the Department of Transportation, within a few years as many as 15 million workers will be "telecommuting." Their workplace will be anyplace that allows them to plug in their computer. From 1992 to 2002, the increase in the number of telecommuters will have skyrocketed by 650 percent. Another significant statistic: In the United States within the next three decades, 50 percent of us will be working in jobs that do not exist today. ("Adapt," as they say, "or die!") Know what you want and pursue it.

As empowered assistants consider the rapid pace of change, they see concomitant opportunities—opportunities for growth, gain, and increased productivity. To be sure, technology-related skills (knowing how to use graphics or spreadsheet software, for example) are important. They will help you get the job. But the other skills I have been stressing will help you *keep* the job. Once you have learned how to do word processing, or use the fax or e-mail tool, you will find the technology skills are insufficient for getting ahead. Your personal and interpersonal skills assume a greater importance as time goes on.

Consider the Internet, expanded from military to public use within the last two decades. In 1982, we had only 235 connected computers. To date, there are over 30 million cyberspace cadets with more signing on daily. Over 30,000 chat groups have been formed. The value of the Internet and localized Intranets is access to information, the most prized commodity in the information era.

The fastest-growing aspect of the Internet is the World Wide Web. Within a few years, there will be over 100 million companies with home pages, accessible to any cyberspace traveler. The Web features text, sound, graphics, and animation, and surfing it is an enjoyable adventure, facilitated by the key words that interconnect all topics.

Experts predict that it will soon be commonplace to find computers with voice recognition capacity, thus eliminating the keyboard as we know it. We already have systems in place able to take dictation of more than 100 words a minute. The dictation is then entered into a word processing program that recognizes the user's voice.

Another fast-approaching reality will be networked PCs available to all employees. Teams will use them to share information with desktop clients who need both input to and output from the teams working on a given project. Another such reality is work flows, sequential tasks turned over to a computer for processing in a consistent fashion. Computer appliances have moved off the horizons and onto our desktops. They are miniature computer enhancements designed for very specific and small-scale tasks.

RISC (reduced instruction set computer) processors will soon work in conjunction with the next generation of Intel processors, built with a cross-over technology that enables the old to work with the new. Considerable excitement surrounds the multimedia advances in the hardware field. Computers themselves will contain what we now see and hear on CD-ROMs. And you have no doubt heard about wireless computing, which allows the users to do virtually any PC function just by walking around with a hand-held device. CBWA (computing by walking around) will no doubt replace MBWA (management by walking around) in short order.

One force driving these changes will be the reversal of industrial age conditions, which call for the assemblage of huge numbers of people in a single location to do manufacturing work. The United States is no longer an industrial nation; more than 75 percent of our workforce is engaged in service organizations rather than industrial manufacturing. Knowledge workers can do their work wherever they can find the knowledge they need. Consequently, SOHO employees (small office/home office) can telecommute via simple dialup connections.

Consider just one example to illustrate the tremendous change facing employees: A shoe store in Westport, Connecticut, has no shoes in stock and yet it is doing a thriving business. How can it be? you wonder. In truth, given the store's computer capacity, it has over 10 million pairs available because each style comes in every possible size. It's just that the shoes don't exist until the customer places an order, which is done by having the buyer's feet scanned electronically. The data are then sent to the shoe manufacturer in Italy via modem. Two weeks later, the custom-made shoes arrive at the customer's door.

Similarly, banks as we know them today will not exist tomorrow. They will be replaced by virtual banks, just as your company in time will be replaced, futurists assert, by virtual offices. To refuse to acknowledge change or to avoid preparing for it is to commit career suicide.

How can you possibly maintain your composure amid these radical transformations? The answer is knowledge, your only hope. In addition to the obvious ways of acquiring knowledge (classes, magazines, user groups, books, self-teaching, conferences, trade shows, product demonstrations), I strongly urge you to find a computer coach. Somewhere in your organization (or in your neighborhood or your friendship cycle) is a technophile—an individual absolutely enamored with technology, a person who cares more about chips embedded in smart cards than chips embedded in cookies.

In this coach-neophyte relationship, you will be giving as much as you get. Make it very clear to the person whose brain you would like to tap that you are willing to offer as much in return as he is willing to share. Your offering will center on whatever needs the other person has. In an office setting, the coach who stops his work in order to answer your questions for half an hour deserves to have half an hour of your time in return. Determine what you can do *before* your tutoring session starts. And then follow through on your promise (to do filing or graphics layout, to make calls or travel arrangements) before you ask for help again.

Your "tekkie"—inside your office or inside your community—has more things to do than time in which to do them. And so you may offer an exchange that deals with babysitting, shopping, gardening, or something else. You must give instead of simply take if you want your technocrat to explain learning that has taken him a long time to acquire. Use this help to discover the knowledge shortcuts and bypass the reading of manuals. Your newly acquired expertise will open entirely new empowerment vistas.

Benchmarking

From the total quality movement comes the word *benchmarking*, which essentially means comparing certain work processes to the processes of others known for their excellence. Beyond the comparison, of course, the insights gleaned from the benchmark must be applied to improve your own operations. You can benchmark with anyone or any one organization. What should your benchmarking study concentrate on? On whatever aspect of your work you would like to improve.

The suggestions that follow will guide you as you undertake a benchmarking project, an ideal forum for demonstrating your desire for and ability to handle greater empowerment.

1. *Determine the work process that can benefit most from a comparison study.* You may wish to confer with your boss, other secretaries, or anyone else committed to the concept of continuous improvement.

2. *Develop a plan.* Detail and quantify the existing process, identify potential benchmarking partners, estimate how long and how costly you anticipate the project to be, and specify the results you hope to attain by engaging in it. Review the barriers you anticipate encountering and the people you wish to have on your benchmarking team. Include a mission statement, and show its relevance to your company's mission statement. Also include the questions you intend to ask your benchmarking partner.

3. *Share the plan with those within your organization whose approval is manda-tory.* Some policies, for example, require going through the public rela-tions department with such a venture, which would have you serving as a representative of your company. The legal department may need to be advised, to ensure you are not disclosing proprietary information. Obtaining all these approvals may seem tiresome, but just think of the visibility you will gain in the process.

4. *Formally contact the other organization you wish to serve as your benchmarking partner.* After sending a letter requesting a site visit, place a phone call to discuss details of your request, explain how the data will be used, and ascertain in what ways you might assist your partner in return for the time they will be spending with you during your visit. Following the phone call, send a list of the questions you intend to ask, along with a brief description of the scope of your benchmarking en-deavor.

5. *Assemble a team.* Your team should consist of four or five members who will visit the partner site. These individuals will have expressed a sin-cere interest in learning about best practices in order to apply that knowledge to improve existing practices within your own organiza-tion. Ideally, team members will be outgoing enough to ask questions, receptive enough to listen to answers, thorough enough to take exten-sive notes, and hardworking enough to translate what was learned into widely shared improvements upon their return.

   Make certain an agreement has been reached in advance concerning such details as how long the visit will last, what will be studied, what materials you will give, what materials you would like to receive, who the contact person will be, and what steps will be taken following the visit. Do your best to stick to the schedule and to be as unobtrusive as possible when entering workstations at the benchmarkee's facility. Afterwards, write a follow-up letter expressing appreciation for the time spent with you. Peri-odically update your partner with information regarding improvements that have been instituted as a result of the site visit.

6. *The essential question during the analysis part of benchmarking is,* "Based on what we've learned, how can we improve?" The findings must be translated into flowcharts, graphs, and narratives—all of which are com-pared to measurements about your own organization. After this data assessment, a summary is written, specifying the opportunities for in-

creased efficiency and productivity. The summary also specifies recommendations for implementation of new methods, concepts, or procedures.

7. Depending on who will be affected by the changes, the *benchmarking team members meet with various individuals throughout the organization to explain what they have learned and what they would like done with this new knowledge.* They detail the anticipated benefits and assist with the implementation in every way they can. Then they determine the receptivity to and readiness for change.

8. *Undertake the improvement and track the results to learn what impact the change is having.* If the results are negligible, the team and those affected assess the value of the instituted changes, calibrating where necessary, perhaps even deciding to abandon the change and return to the former way of conducting business.

If the results reveal the change is having a positive impact on operations (and this is the typical outcome), the team and involved others meet to discuss how to extend the new procedures to other parts of the organization. The more widely communicated the successes are, the more likely the changes can be institutionalized.

Answers to the Case Studies on Pages 103 and 104

Case Study 1. Our business consultants—Trish Rintels, former vice president of production for Blake Edwards Entertainment and currently on the "mommy track" in Charlottesville, Virginia; Linda Edison, cofounder of Edison International in Oneonta, New York; and Germaine Froelich, Information Technology Resource Specialist for the City School District of Rochester, New York—think that answer b is the best choice for Cynthia. If she follows option a, she will not only be doing something at which she is not particularly talented, but establishing a pattern calling for her to do the same kind of task in the future. If she is truly interested in optimizing the team's work, she should ask for an assignment more in line with her talents. In the honest and open environments in which most teams operate, the team leader will probably appreciate her forthright response. Remember that she is not refusing to pitch in, she is merely asking that her contribution be maximized.

Option c has a drawback too. If Cynthia, who is not especially skilled with metrics, is teamed with someone who is, the expert will probably find her efficiency diminished by virtue of having to explain a number of things to Cynthia along the way. Why have two people doing the job that one could do alone, and more efficiently?

Case Study 2. Our experts felt that Nancy should direct the customer to her supervisor's boss (option c). By following choice a, Nancy would be passing up a rare opportunity: having someone in upper management made aware of Nancy's outstanding qualities. Option b is not realistic; most customers impressed with good service are willing to take a few moments then and there to express their appreciation but are not willing to take time to write a letter afterwards.

Case Study 3. The consensus for this case study focused on Juana's actually meeting with the executive assistant (option a), explaining the circumstances, and asking to be considered for the position when it is announced. Employees who are leaving an organization often have considerable input into the decision about who will replace them, and so Juana will have an advantage by putting in her bid early with the assistant. The second choice may or may not make Juana noticed by those in the executive offices. And if she goes with option c, it may be too late. By the time the announcement is officially made, the decision may have been made as well.

Case Study 4. Lisa, our consultants felt, should advise the boss to wait (option c). The problem may not really be a problem; also, the manager has already been advised that the boss is wondering if there are grounds for a harassment charge to be filed. The suspected manager—guilty or innocent—would be foolish to engage in unprofessional behavior at this point. Outright refusal (option a) may cause Lisa some difficulty in her relationship with her boss. On the other hand, going along with a plan that troubles her morally (option b) is wrong as well.

The boss has understandable and legitimate concerns for the welfare of employees and also for the company's financial position (lawsuits can be devastating). However, asking a subordinate to spy is an underhanded means of solving the problem. If it was ever learned that Lisa had participated in such a scheme, her reputation among colleagues would certainly be tarnished.

Tips from Terrance Keys, Assistant Director, Educational Technology Services/Professional Development Monroe Community College

The workplace is changing and new technologies are an important part of these changes. If you do not prepare for them, you will soon find that you no longer have the skills necessary for your job. Below are some strategies you can use to help prepare for the changes that are coming.

- *Attend training sessions.* If your company offers professional development courses, attend them. If it does not, look into local training companies or community education courses. Often, your company will pay for your training if you prove your interest and use what you learn to improve your job performance.

- *Read magazines.* Subscribe to one of the many technology-specific publications. There are titles for all levels of users (including nonusers). The next best thing to using the technology is reading about it, because then you are at least aware of what is coming. You can be the one suggesting new technologies for your company to use.

- *Learn the terms.* If you know the acronyms and terms common in technology, you will be able to ask intelligent questions and understand the answers. The easiest way to learn the terms is to follow this rule: Read! Read! Read!

- *Ask questions.* If you are not sure how to do something, you must ask questions and write down the answers. I never mind answering questions from people who are interested in improving their skills, but I do mind answering the same questions repeatedly. The same thing applies to help desks. In order to keep track of the answers, start a technology notebook in which you write notes, hints, shortcuts, and any other related information.

- *Attend conferences.* Conferences are a great way to see what the future holds or what others are doing today. Most major cities have technology-related conferences sponsored by colleges, corporations, or user groups. Many are inexpensive or even free. Call a local computer store, and ask if there are any new technology demonstrations coming soon. Join a professional society or a user group, and attend the meetings.

- *Explore the Internet.* The Internet is becoming a common means of communication and information exchange. Information is one of the most important commodities in business today, and the Internet offers a wealth of it. If you know how to access information on the Internet, you will be a valuable asset to your company. There are on-line magazines that can help you stay up-to-date as well.

- *Experiment.* Try doing something a new way. See what that menu option does. Try to find a more efficient way to work. People often learn one way to do things and never look for others. Each new version of software features shortcuts and tools designed to save you time. Try them.

- *Be open to new technology.* The most important way you can prepare for the future is to be open to it. This means you should accept the technology offered to you and try to learn what it can do. If you are interested in learning what is available and applying it to your job, you are a valuable asset to your company.

- *Take your office into the twenty-first century.* Start your personal transformation as you acquire knowledge about both existing and imminent developments: complete and constant connectivity; office suites (a single computer with word processing, spreadsheet, database, presentation, mail, graphing, scanning, digital cameras, write-able compact disks, appliances, and clip art capacities—all in one!); and a work environment with flexible workspaces, "brainstorming" and "hoteling" space (telecommuting employees call in to reserve office space for themselves and others), PC portability, voice recognition, and artificial intelligence (the computer learns from you).

In Conclusion

As you no doubt realize—having read this book, done the exercises, thought about the challenges presented, and having learned from the interviewees—the times they are a-changin'. Who will survive the change? Who will thrive on it? The person who not only welcomes it but who invites it into her life!

How do you go about transforming yourself from a change-fearful to a change-receptive secretary? You become a continual learner. You read, you take courses, you learn as much as you can about the perpetually changing and rapidly changing face of business today. You improve your organizational and communications skills; you establish your authority for taking an empowered stance; you develop your ability to maintain composure no matter what circumstances erupt as, along with the rest of us, you move from the "nanosecond nineties" into a new millennium. In short, you ground yourself against future shock by preparing for the future.

One of the most powerful forces driving change is the climate of empowerment, a climate that says to *all* employees, "We need what you have to contribute." No matter who you are, what position you hold, or where you work, you have to report to somebody. In an empowered culture, though, you have greater control than ever before over your job and the intelligent execution of it. Why is this so important? Why does it present such great opportunity?

Empowerment is vital for both corporate and personal well-being. For you as an individual, having greater control over your work and having influence on the decisions that impact your job mean less stress. In a recently concluded longitudinal study of 12,500 Swedish employees, it was found that when workers were given greater control over their own jobs, they experienced less stress and less damage to their heart. Less stress, not surprisingly, equates with a happier work environment, which equates with better and more work being done. (The World Health Organization estimates that stress costs American organizations $200 billion a year in mistakes, bad decisions, accidents, lost time, illness, litigation, and lower productivity.)

In this fourteen-year study, low-control working conditions were found to be a leading risk factor for heart disease. But not just the individual suffers when she fails to seek empowerment or when managers fail to give it. The organization suffers too. Studies show improvement in quality, service, and productivity—gains of 50 percent and higher—when employees are empowered to do what they believe is right.

Apart from health issues for the individual and profit issues for the company, as a secretary you gain numerous other benefits from asserting your authority and independence. Empowerment provides opportunities to demonstrate your capabilities; it offers you the challenge of new conditions; it fosters the pride that comes with ownership. Further, in an empowered workplace, you save time by not having to obtain approval for every action. Micromanaging is out; trust is in. Today's efficiency-driven manager is guided by the words of General George S. Patton: "Give direction, not directions." The new manager is learning to trust the intelligence of secretaries, who, in turn, are learning to take on more and more managerial tasks.

In such circumstances, communications flow more readily and individuals are valued for what they can *do*, not for the titles that follow their names. Problems are solved collectively; the mission itself becomes the boss; and new relationships are formed as management looks at empowered secretaries in a new light.

The current business climate, propelled by forces such as the decimation of middle-management positions and the convenience of telecommuting, means growth. With more duties comes greater opportunity—opportunity to treat your job as if it were your own business, opportunity to grow, to learn, to exert greater control over the various components that constitute your work life.

But responsibility, like trust, is a two-way street. Managers who assume that empowerment means "power to the people" have the responsibility of explaining how that power will be used (this is where the 5-In Model comes in). Empty phrases such as "do whatever it takes" leave the secretary wondering exactly what empowerment means. Managers need to assist employees in taking at first small, then greater steps to autonomy. They need to assure themselves and numerous others that empowerment should not be regarded as "turning the asylum over to the inmates."

Secretaries, of course, also have a responsibility—to go beyond the ordinary ways of doing work, solving problems, making decisions. Sometimes they are reluctant to accept greater responsibility because they feel they were not hired to do anything beyond their job description. But the secretary, such as you, who is reading a book on this topic, does not fall into the "it's not my job" category of employees. The secretary seeking power over her job does not merely follow instructions—she helps determine what those instructions should be.

In the empowered workplace, employees are not asked if they wish to be empowered but rather to what extent they will be empowered. For most, such a workplace offers exciting possibilities. To be sure, fear will occasionally poke its head through the empowerment-opened door. But experience and small successes will soon make the newly empowered secretary an advocate of empowerment for all.

For those of you intent on developing your personal portfolio through investment in empowerment projects, let me offer my admiration and this wish: More power to you!

Bibliography

Alberti, Robert E., and Michael L. Emmons. *Your Perfect Right: A Guide to Assertive Behavior.* San Luis Obispo, Calif.: Impact Publishers, 1980.

American Society for Training and Development. Alexandria, Va. *Training and Development.*

Bell, Chip. *Managers as Mentors.* San Francisco: Barrett-Koehler Publishers, 1996.

Bernstein, Albert J., and Sydney Craft Rozen. *Dinosaur Brains.* New York: Ballantine Books, 1989.

Block, Peter. *Stewardship.* San Francisco: Publishers Group, 1996.

Cetron, Marvin. *Probable Tomorrows.* New York: St. Martin's Press, 1997.

DePree, Max. *Leadership Is an Art.* Garden City, N.Y.: Doubleday, 1989.

Doyle, Michael, and David Strauss. *How to Make Meetings Work.* New York: Berkley Publishing Group, 1982.

Fromm, Bill, and Len Schlesinger. *The Real Heroes of Business and Not a CEO Among Them.* New York: Bantam Doubleday, 1993.

Handy, Charles. *The Age of Paradox.* Boston: Harvard Business School Press, 1994.

Imai, Masaaki. *Kaizen: The Key to Japan's Competitive Success.* New York: Random House, 1986.

Johnson, Spencer. *"Yes" or "No": The Guide to Better Decisions.* New York: HarperCollins, 1992.

Kaufman, Paul, and Cindy Wetmore. *The Brass Tacks Manager: How to Shoot from the Hip Without Shooting Yourself in the Foot.* Garden City, N.Y.: Doubleday, 1994.

Larsen, Earnie, and Jeanette Goodstein. *Who's Driving Your Bus? Codependent Business Behaviors of Workaholics, Perfectionists, Martyrs, Tap Dancers, Caretakers, and People Pleasers.* San Diego: Pfeiffer & Company, 1993.

Lizotte, Ken, and Barbara A. Litwak. *From Secretary Track to Fast Track.* New York: AMACOM, 1996.

Packard, Vance. *The Hidden Persuaders.* New York: Pocket Books, 1981.

Peters, Tom. *The Pursuit of Wow! Every Person's Guide to Topsy-Turvy Times.* New York: Random House, 1994.

Sherman, Stephanie, and V. Clayton Sherman. *Make Yourself Memorable.* New York: AMACOM, 1996.

Stroman, J., and K. Wilson. *Administrative Assistant's and Secretary's Handbook.* New York: AMACOM, 1995.

Tingley, Judith C. *Say What You Mean/Get What You Want.* New York: AMACOM, 1996.

Tuckman, B. W., and M. A. C. Jensen. "Stages of Small Group Development Revisited." *Group and Organizational Studies*, Vol. 2: No. 4 (1977), pp. 419–427.

Index